Patti Silverman and Pamela Dee

SOUND OF MANY WATERS

And His Voice was Like the Sound of Many Waters;
and the Earth Shone with His Glory

ACW Press
Nashville, TN 37222

Sound of Many Waters
Copyright ©2008 Patti Silverman
All rights reserved

Cover Design by Alpha Advertising
Interior design by Pine Hill Graphics

Packaged by ACW Press
PO Box 110390
Nashville, TN 37222
www.acwpress.com
The views expressed or implied in this work do not necessarily reflect those of ACW Press. Ultimate design, content, and editorial accuracy of this work is the responsibility of the author(s).

Publisher's Cataloging-in-Publication Data
(Provided by Cassidy Cataloguing Services, Inc.)
Silverman, Patti.

    Sound of many waters : and His voice was like the sound of many waters, and the earth shone with his glory / Patti Silverman and Pamela Dee. -- 1st ed. -- Nashville, TN : ACW Press, 2008.

    p. ; cm.
    ISBN: 978-1-932124-37-8

    1. Devotional calendars. 2. Devotional literature. 3. Bible Meditations. I. Dee, Pamela. II. Title.

BV4810 .S55 2008
242/.2--dc22   0801

Printed in the United States of America.

Acknowledgments

There were many fellow servants in this work, known by name to the Lord. May He richly bless them all for their sacrifice and faithfulness.

To the true oracles of God who submit
their lives to be human vessels of the pure
word of the Lord.

A true oracle will never speak except what
God speaks, because he speaks through a
completely risen spirit. There is no mental
input, letting logic or reason control the
word. The mark of a true oracle is the Father
within him has His way, has His say, has His
sway. A true oracle will reflect who God is
and tell you things to come.

And

To Pamela Dee, a companion in the Lord who
gave her life to uphold the pure word of God.

Foreword

There is a deluge of daily devotionals on the Christian market, but I am bold enough to say this book is unique. It contains the whole word of God, without man's interpretation.

We invite the reader to savor these pearls of great price and allow the Holy Spirit free reign in your heart to imprint the nature of Christ there in all His glory.

God's word is a vast treasury which is unending, as infinite as the Lord Himself. We are instructed in Matthew 4:4 to live by every word that proceeds from the mouth of God. This is a present tense, ongoing *proceeding*, as limitless as God is limitless. All the wisdom of the ages, the universe, the creation, is contained in the persons of the Father, the Son, and the Holy Spirit. We have only to sit at His feet and learn of Him.

God says, "You must know that there is no other way that you will grow in this last day, than to feed on the *logos* (written word) and the *rhema* (spoken word), because it is that two-edged sword which will cause the work to be done against the enemy. The enemy fears mightily those who walk in *logos* and *rhema*, and those who are trained in that."

"The entire word, both written and yet to be spoken, is contained in the Person of the Son. I want My sons to live by every word that proceeds out of My mouth. Have I not called My beloved Son, Jesus, the Word?"

January 1

God says, "I, the Lord, would have you know I love you. I, the Lord, would have you know I care for you. I have your personal needs in My concern. My love for you is great. Surely I will meet your needs. I will endeavor to hold you when the tempter comes and tries to deliver you out of the hand of the Lord. The Lord will deal with him, and the Lord will rebuke him."

> *"Israel was holiness to the Lord, the firstfruits of His increase. All that devour him will offend; disaster will come upon them, says the Lord."*
> Jeremiah 2:3

God says, "Come, the Lord loves you. The Lord believes in you. The Lord can save you. The Lord will deliver you. The Lord will heal you. The Lord will forgive you and restore you."

> *"He makes me lie down in [fresh, tender] green pastures; He leads me beside the still and restful waters. He refreshes and restores my life...He leads me in the paths of righteousness...for His name's sake."* Psalm 23:2-3 (AMP)

January 2

God says, "Reach out and take My hand, My children. Take My hand now. Hold on as tight as you can, for I'll hold you tighter. Love Me with all your heart, for I love you more. I love you, My children, I love you, I love you, I love you."

"For I the Lord your God hold your right hand;
I am the Lord, Who says to you, Fear not; I will
help you!" Isaiah 41:13 (AMP)

You are so very special to God!

"...I have called you by your name; you are
Mine. Since you were precious in My sight, you
have been honored, and I have loved you..."
Isaiah 43:1b, 4a

How much more special could special be?

January 3

God says, "I love you, and I will live in you gladly this day and in every day to come. Invite Me in each day. Ask Me to come into your life, for I love you."

"For you are a holy people to the Lord your God, and the Lord has chosen you to be a people for Himself, a special treasure above all the peoples who are on the face of the earth.'"
Deuteronomy 14:2

"God is our refuge and strength, a very present help in trouble." Psalm 46:1

God says, "I shall seek those only who are dedicated to Me and My precepts, those who seek Me early and late, those who meditate and seek Me. Those who pour out their hearts to Me, I will comfort, for I shall comfort them that long after My ways, and I shall fill them with the joy and the reward of fulfillment. I will fulfill the desires of their heart, and I will be their mainstay in a world of uncertainty."

"Now to Him who is able to do exceedingly abundantly above all that we ask or think, according to the power that works in us."
Ephesians 3:20

January 4

"We love Him because He first loved us."
1 John 4:19

"For this is the love of God, that we keep His commandments. And His commandments are not burdensome." 1 John 5:3

God asks, "Do you love Me more than your own mind, your own ambitions, your own opinions, your own resolutions, your own affirmations? Do you love Me enough to leave your nets and follow Me?" (See Matthew 4:18-22.)

God says, "I will never stop loving you even if you stop loving Me."

"But God, who is rich in mercy, because of His great love with which He loved us, even when we were dead in trespasses, made us alive together with Christ..." Ephesians 2:4-5

January 5

God says, "Let love be your greatest aim, as My *logos* says. Love is the love you can begin with as My love. You are, after all, an extension of My love, an extension of My Son."

"Beloved, if God so loved us, we also ought to love one another...if we love one another, God abides in us, and His love has been perfected in us." 1 John 4:11-12

God says, "Let your love be unconditional. Let your heart be softened, and let it be turned into a heart of flesh which will be a heart of love beyond your understanding. Treat one another so softly, so kindly, as though Christ were dealing with them; and you shall see an increase in all I give you."

"Love suffers long and is kind; love does not envy; love does not parade itself, is not puffed up; does not behave rudely, does not seek its own, is not provoked, thinks no evil; does not rejoice in iniquity, but rejoices in the truth; bears all things, believes all things, hopes all things, endures all things. Love never fails..."
1 Corinthians 13:4-8a

January 6

God says, "I fill your heart with the greatest amount of love that you can bear, and you must want all the love I can give you until you cannot hold anymore."

"For I am persuaded that neither death nor life, nor angels nor principalities nor powers, nor things present nor things to come, nor height nor depth...shall be able to separate us from the love of God which is in Christ Jesus our Lord."
Romans 8:38-39

God says, "I want to love you until I am full in you, until there is none of you and all of Me. Let Me fill you with Myself. Let Me fill you with My love."

"Behold what manner of love the Father has bestowed on us, that we should be called children of God...." 1 John 3:1a

January 7

God says, "As you surrender each area of your life that's not of Me, I will crucify it. I love you. I urge you and compel you by My love, not by My mighty force."

God will not ask anything of you in love without knowing you can do it.

"The Lord has appeared of old to me, saying:
'Yes, I have loved you with an everlasting love;
therefore with lovingkindness I have drawn you."
Jeremiah 31:3

God says, "Surely the Lord God is with you. Surely the Lord God loves you. Surely the Lord God is hovering over you by His Spirit. Surely He will allow you to do all things He commands you to do. Surely He will manifest His presence with you. Surely He will meet you when you need Him. Surely He will be there in the quiet hour when you are listening for Him. He would say unto you this day, 'Be My ambassadors. Represent Me where you are and where you go.'"

"And He said, 'My presence will go with you,
and I will give you rest.'" Exodus 33:14

January 8

God says, "I always show you love, in spite of My correction. And when I sent My Son to die, do you think it's a small matter for Me to allow Him to die for you when He was not guilty of anything?"

"For the love of Christ compels us... and He died for all, that those who live should live no longer for themselves, but for Him who died for them and rose again." 2 Corinthians 5:14a,15

God says, "I am trying to get you to see that I love you, and that My love is also refining. My love loves you so much I will not permit you to walk in error knowingly; that when I alert you to error, that you will be loving enough toward My Son to want to correct His body, because it's not your body. It's Christ's church."

"I will keep your law continually, forever and ever [hearing, receiving, loving, and obeying it]. And I will walk at liberty and at ease, for I have sought and inquired for [and desperately required] Your precepts." Psalm 119:44-45 (AMP)

January 9

God says, "I am love, and you are created to be loved by Me and to love Me back. You must come in intimacy to Me. You must be love. You must not say you love. You must be love, for God is love. Love unqualifiedly. Love unconditionally. Love with all your heart. Love with the earnest of your intentions."

> *"And walk in love, as Christ also has loved us and given Himself for us, an offering and a sacrifice to God for a sweet-smelling aroma."*
> Ephesians 5:2

> *"If I then, your Lord and Teacher, have washed your feet, you also ought to wash one another's feet."* John 13:14

Two great commandments Christ gave were to love God with all your heart, mind, soul, and strength and then love each other as yourself. (See Matthew 22:37,39.)

God says, "If you do not have a good appraisal of yourself or value of yourself, you will not learn how to love another person."

> *"But by the grace of God I am what I am, and His grace toward me was not in vain..."*
> 1 Corinthians 15:10a

January 10

Our world changes people, then loves them. God loves us first, and along the way, because we are loved, we are changed.

"In this is love, not that we loved God, but that He loved us and sent His Son to be the propitiation for our sins." 1 John 4:10

God says, "Never forget the three powerful resources you always have available to you: God's unconditional love, prayer, and forgiveness."

"...and as He had loved those who were His own in the world, He loved them to the last and to the highest degree." John 13:1 (AMP)

"But there is forgiveness with You [just what man needs], that You may be reverently feared and worshiped." Psalm 130:4 (AMP)

January 11

God says, "The first law of liberty is the love law of *agape*, God's love. Love knows no boundaries. Love knows no racial lines. Love knows no 'but this' or 'but that.' Love is not a mistake. The unlove is the mistake."

> *"And may the Lord make you to increase and*
> *excel and overflow in love for one another and*
> *for all people, just as we also do for you."*
> 1 Thessalonians 3:12

God says, "God has loved you since He existed because He is love. He loved you before you loved Him. He loved you in the womb. He loved you before the world began. There was no beginning to His love for you, and there is no end to it."

> *"And we have known and believed the love God*
> *has for us. God is love, and he who abides in*
> *love abides in God, and God in him."*
> 1 John 4:16

January 12

God says, "I want your heart to open up today and receive the goodness and love of God, for My love casts out all fear, for perfect love has no torment."

"There is no fear in love; but perfect love casts out fear, because fear involves torment..."
1 John 4:18a

God says, "Enlarge your heart to take God in. God does not say this to reproach or condemn us, for we are nested in His heart where we are to remain."

"Surely or only goodness, mercy and unfailing love shall follow me all the days of my life, and through the length of my days the house of the Lord [and His presence] shall be my dwelling place." Psalm 23:6 (AMP)

January 13

God says, "I love you. I'll love you forever. I will never stop loving you, even if you fail Me, but why would you want to fail Me? A perfect God, a loving God, a God that means only the best for you. Don't fail Me, because I won't fail you."

"Answer me speedily, O Lord; my spirit fails! Do not hide Your face from me, lest I be like those who go down into the pit. Cause me to hear Your lovingkindness in the morning, for in You I do trust; cause me to know the way in which I should walk, for I lift up my soul to You." Psalm 143:7-8

"Love never fails..." 1 Corinthians 13:8a

God asks, "What will you do when there is nothing but your God and you standing alone naked, in the garden? What will you say, or what will you do when you know that your defense is totally on God's reserve love and unfathomable love nature of grace He bestows on those who even have a glimmer of truth?"

"Then the Lord God called to Adam and said to him, 'Where are you?' So he said, 'I heard your voice in the garden, and I was afraid because I was naked; and I hid myself.'"
Genesis 3:9-10

January 14

God asks, "What keeps you from yielding to Me today? Why are you still drawn back when you know all I want to do is love you? All I want to do is cradle you. All I want to do is protect you. All I want to do is take away the fear, the anxiety, the care. All I want to do is release you from the world."

"Now do not be stiff-necked,...but yield yourselves to the Lord; and enter His sanctuary, which He has sanctified forever, and serve the Lord your God..." 2 Chronicles 30:8

God says, "I always show you love in spite of My chastisement. True love corrects. True love will put the Lord first. True love will insist the principles of God will be observed in the home."

"He who disdains instruction despises his own soul, but he who heeds reproof gets understanding." Proverbs 15:32

"For whom the Lord loves He chastens, and scourges every son whom He receives." Hebrews 12:6

January 15

God says, "If you knew how much I loved you, you would love Me at least in some measure. You'd put away your toys, and you would relinquish all your control that I may glorify My Son in you; for I, your heavenly Father, am coming back in My Son. Be ready and receive Me, My people, for I am coming soon."

Christ said, "Father, I desire that they also whom You gave Me may be with Me where I am, that they may behold My glory which you have given Me; for You loved Me before the foundation of the world. And I have declared to them Your name, and will declare it, that the love with which You loved Me may be in them, and I in them." John 17:24,26

God says, "A man with a double eye sees mixed signals, double vision, and will always be enticed by that which is not of Me. I do not entice. I am a compelling, loving Father."

"The lamp of the body is the eye. Therefore, when your eye is good, your whole body also is full of light. But when your eye is bad, your body also is full of darkness. Therefore take heed that the light which is in you is not darkness."
Luke 11:34-35

January 16

God says, "By faith receive My love, for you are saved by that love, and faith came into you, because you saw Me there in that lonely place where you knew you needed Me, for I came and tugged on your heart, and you released to Me the heart of care that I cleansed, and the spirit I renewed. Come and surrender. Come and surrender to Me."

"But whoever keeps His word, truly the love of God is perfected in him. By this we know that we are in Him." 1 John 2:5

"My soul longs, yes, even faints for the courts of the Lord; my heart and my flesh cry out for the living God." Psalm 84:2

God says, "Do not be afraid, for there is nothing to fear. Perfect love casts out fear, for fear has torment. Accept My love today and dote upon each other. The love I have given you, give to one another. Share that love, because that love is the greatest weapon you can have against the army of Satan."

"And above all things have fervent love for one another, for 'love will cover a multitude of sins.'" 1 Peter 4:8

January 17

God $says,$ "The Lord is in His holy place. Bow your knee before Me, and your heart. Let your heart not be proud before Me because of what you think you've accomplished. In the Lord, you accomplish much when you reach out to each other, when you love as I love, when you humble yourself before one another. When you're in one accord, then My angels will dance with joy."

"From whom the whole body, joined and knit together by what every joint supplies, according to the effective working by which every part does its share, causes growth of the body for the edifying of itself in love." Ephesians 4:16

God $says,$ "Look on the heart in one another, not the outward man. See each other as completed works of God."

"But the Lord said to Samuel, 'Do not look at his appearance...for the Lord does not see as man sees; for man looks at the outward appearance, but the Lord looks at the heart.'"
1 Samuel 16:7

January 18

God says, "I am with you always—even to the end of this age, and My Spirit will go with you. I will be there when you need Me." (See Hebrews 13:5b.)

So you say: "God's Spirit is with me always—even to the end of this age. His Spirit goes with me and will be there when I need Him." Amen!

God says, "Come today, and set your face like flintstone, and see the Lord comes. This principle is the principle of hope, faith, and love—and faith and love are good; but love will conquer all hope and faith. Love is the greatest of all things. That's the mystery unveiled. The love of God is always there for all people, be they murderers, be they good, be they bad."

"... 'Now we believe, not because of what you said, for we have heard for ourselves and know that this is indeed the Christ, the Savior of the world.'" John 4:42

January 19

The encouraging truth about the spiritual life is that you're never alone. God provides His resources to help you in the process. He won't make decisions for you or do what you are able to do, but He does work in ways known and unknown to help you become like Christ.

"Behold, I am with you and will keep you wherever you go, and will bring you back to this land; for I will not leave you until I have done what I have spoken to you." Genesis 28:15

God says, "I am able. I am able. I am able. I shall not fail thee. As darkness descends, I ascend. As light diminishes, My light increases, and as despair goes, hope grows."

"Therefore He is also able to save to the uttermost those who come to God through Him, since He ever lives to make intercession for them." Hebrews 7:25

"Now to Him who is able to keep you from stumbling, and to present you faultless before the presence of His glory with exceeding joy."
Jude 24

January 20

Edification means to build up one's spiritual growth.

God says, "The fruit of edification is to know God is who He says He is, and we are who God says we are."

> *"Therefore let us pursue the things which make for peace and the things by which one may edify another."* Romans 14:19

God says, "Be excited about the Lord Jesus Christ. He is the excitement of excitements. He is the crown of My kingdom. He is the King. He is the Lord. He is the God. He is the Healer. He's the Creator. He's the Perfecter. He is the One who has completed it. Behold, it is finished, saith the Lord."

> *"Now may the God of peace...make you complete in every good work to do His will, working in you what is well pleasing in His sight, through Jesus Christ..."* Hebrews 13:20-21

January 21

God says, "In moments of severe suffering when you think all is lost, you come into the presence of God, and all is gained. Nothing is lost."

"Yet indeed I also count all things loss for the excellence of the knowledge of Christ Jesus my Lord, for whom I have suffered the loss of all things, and count them as rubbish, that I may gain Christ." Philippians 3:8

God says, "Let your heart ring with the knowledge that I have brought peace and love and joy, and I will leave it with you to maintain it from now on. Do not lose what I have given you, for I am the truth, the way, the resurrection life, and I am your way to eternity."

"Therefore, having been justified by faith, we have peace with God through our Lord Jesus Christ." Romans 5:1

"Now hope does not disappoint, because the love of God has been poured out in our hearts by the Holy Spirit who was given to us."
Romans 5:5

January 22

God says, "I want you to be in the stream of My blessing."

"...and I will cause showers to come down in their season; there shall be showers of blessing."
Ezekiel 34:26b

"Blessed be the God and Father of our Lord Jesus Christ, who has blessed us with every spiritual blessing in the heavenly places in Christ."
Ephesians 1:3

God says, "Jesus, Jesus, Jesus. That name is far above every name both in heaven and on earth. That name will deliver you from any predicament you find yourself in, in this earth life. That name is the name mightiest of all names; and when I hear that name from the heart of a believer, I send My angels instantly to minister to them."

"And His name, through faith in His name, has made this man strong, whom you see and know. Yes, the faith which comes through Him has given him this perfect soundness in the presence of you all." Acts 3:16

January 23

God says, "And so be content in whatever circumstance you find yourself. As Apostle Paul wrote, 'I've learned to be content in all those circumstances I find myself, in the Spirit of God.'"

"...for I have learned in whatever state I am, to be content: I know how to be abased, and I know how to abound. Everywhere and in all things I have learned both to be full and to be hungry, both to abound and to suffer need. I can do all things through Christ who strengthens me." Philippians 4:11-13

God says, "You must settle it in your heart today. Are you Mine? If you're Mine, do not despair. Do not worry. Do not be troubled. Do not be anxious for anything, for your Father knows the things you have need of."

"Be anxious for nothing, but by everything by prayer and supplication, with thanksgiving, let your requests be made known to God."

Philippians 4:6

January 24

God says, "The joy I've given you will make you whole. The love I give you will lift your soul. I'll give you joy and love. I'll fill your hearts with tranquility, and you will rest and know that I am God. Seek that rest today."

> *"You will show me the path of life; in Your presence is fullness of joy; at Your right hand are pleasures forevermore."* Psalm 16:11

> *"Let us therefore be zealous and exert ourselves and strive diligently to enter that rest [of God, to know and experience it for ourselves]."*
> Hebrews 4:11a (AMP)

God says, "I'm looking for those who are not beholden by men or honored by men, but who are great in their proclivity to cling to Me in good times and in bad."

> *"For do I now persuade men, or God? Or do I seek to please men? For if I still pleased men, I would bot be a servant of Christ."* Galatians 1:10

> *"Now godliness with contentment is great gain."*
> 1 Timothy 6:6

January 25

God says, "Do not try to rush My will. My will is sure, certain, and you can count on it. But let Me do it My way; and though your life may get harsh at times, and you may get disheartened, do not fear. I have overcome the world, and I have overcome it for you, My beloved."

"For whatever is born of God overcomes the world. And this is the victory that has overcome the world—our faith. Who is he who overcomes the world, but he who believes that Jesus is the Son of God?" 1 John 5:4-5

God says, "You presume on Me. You prejudge Me. You determine what will happen, when it will happen, and why it will happen. Only the Spirit can say what, and why, and when, and how. So learn to wait upon the Lord."

"Come now, you who say, 'Today or tomorrow we will go to such and such a city, spend a year there, buy and sell, make a profit'; whereas you do not know what will happen tomorrow. For what is your life? It is even a vapor that appears for a little time and then vanishes away. Instead you ought to say, 'If the Lord wills, we shall live and do this or that.'" James 4:13-15

January 26

God says, "I want the word to become flesh within you, because every time you let it become flesh in you, you'll rise a little higher in My kingdom. You'll know a little more by revelation. Your faith will increase, your contentment will be great, and you will enter My rest."

> *"And the word became flesh and dwelt among us..."* John 1:14a

> *"I will give you a new heart and put a new spirit within you; I will take the heart of stone out of your flesh and give you a heart of flesh. I will put My Spirit within you and cause you to walk in My statutes..."* Ezekiel 36:26-27

God says He longs for us to reach this place...

God says, "Then you will not have reason to have any form of entertainment but Me. Your pleasure is your entertainment—pleasure in you and Me, joined as one."

> *"But test and prove all things [until you can recognize] what is good; [to that] hold fast. Abstain from evil [shrink from it and keep aloof from it] in whatever form or whatever kind it may be."* 1 Thessalonians 5:21-22 (AMP)

January 27

God says, "What is liberty, but breathing the air of My presence, spiritually speaking, and sensing your spirit rising."

"And raised us up together, and made us sit together in the heavenly places in Christ Jesus."
Ephesians 2:6

Liberty in God is freedom of access to the Spirit of God as we rise in our spirits above the carnal plane.

God says, "You have the prerogative to walk only where freedom is. What greater freedom is there than to know you are not walking in sin, than to have no guilt?"

"And you will know the truth, and the truth will set you free. So if the Son liberates you [makes you free men], then you are really and unquestionably free." John 8:32,36 (AMP)

We are to live as free people in a land of bondage.

January 28

We know God is going to erase all the sins and hurts of His people by their own desire to be free.

We recognize our smallness and God's greatness.

"In [this] freedom Christ has made us free [and completely liberated us]; stand fast then, and do not be hampered and held ensnared and submit again to a yoke of slavery [which you have once put off]." Galatians 5:1 (AMP)

God says, "Where the Spirit of the Lord is, there is liberty; and sometimes where the Spirit of the Lord is there, is liberty through purging, through admonition, through chastening. But it is all in perfect love, do not forget."

"My son, do not despise the chastening of the Lord, nor detest His correction; for whom the Lord loves He corrects, just as a father the son in whom he delights." Proverbs 3:11-12

January 29

God says, "So many are not free, even though I've liberated them. They're still bound by their self. They're bound by their flesh. Let go, My people. Let go and be cleansed today, for your God is on the way. He's at your heart's door right now. He is seeking to come in."

> *"Thus says the Lord: stand by the roads and look; and ask for the eternal paths, where the good, old way is; then walk in it, and you will find rest for your souls..."* Jeremiah 6:16a (AMP)

It's your choice but choose wisely. Christ wants to crown you with liberty. Ask yourself, "Is Christ Jesus shackled in my life?"

> *"And I will bring the blind by a way they did not know; I will lead them in paths they have not known. I will make darkness light before them, and crooked places straight. These things I will do for them, and not forsake them."*
> Isaiah 42:16

January 30

God asks, "May you be led by your spirit in praise so your mind is not in it. May you just explode with the love of God in you. You cannot stop, and you don't care if everybody looks at you as peculiar. You are called peculiar by God, so be peculiar. Be as peculiar as you can be today. Let even the remnant look at you strangely. Shout in abandonment."

"In regard to these, they think it strange that you do not run with them in the same flood of dissipation, speaking evil for you." 1 Peter 4:4

God says, "Be free by being free from entanglements you've made in your lives. To be free is to be free in Me. Let your spirit free."

"For you, brethren, were [indeed] called to freedom...through love you should serve one another." Galatians 5:13 (AMP)

January 31

God says, "The only true freedom you will ever have in this world is abandoning yourself to Me, giving Me your whole life as I gave you My Son. I want your life for Myself."

"Now the Lord is the Spirit; and where the Spirit of the Lord is, there is liberty."
2 Corinthians 3:17

"And everyone who has left houses or brothers or sisters or father or mother or wife or children or lands, for My name's sake, shall receive a hundredfold, and inherit eternal life."
Matthew 19:29

God says, "When you are bound in captivity, My children, the walls and bars of your captivity are of your own making because you have not listened and received the word that gives life when it says, 'Whom the Son sets free is free indeed.'"

"...and find Me when you search for Me with all your heart. I will be found by you, says the Lord, and I will release you from captivity..."
Jeremiah 29:13-14 (AMP)

February 1

God says, "These walls of iniquity have held many of you so long you think you're normal. You think you're doing it the way God wants; but when you examine what God says, He does not say that. He does not say that. He says just the opposite. He says, 'Come. Be ready.' When I say 'Come,' come, for the bride that is slovenly, the bride who is wrinkled and with spot or blemish will not be ready."

Crucifixion of the flesh calls for humility.

> *"And after He had appeared in human form, He abased and humbled Himself [still further] and carried His obedience to the extreme of death, even the death of the cross!"* Philippians 2:8 (AMP)

God says, "I will exalt Myself in you, not you in Me, and I will bring down the mighty, and I will raise up the humble, for I have told you before, that pride goes before a sudden destruction. So, be not proud in yourselves, of what you have, or who you are, or what you are, for in Christ Jesus, who are you, really, but a child of God? And if a child, than an heir, an heir of God, and a joint heir with Christ."

> *"The Lord lifts up the humble; He casts the wicked down to the ground."* Psalm 147:6

February 2

God says, "Why do you think about yourself? Yourself is not mentioned in My holy word. Myself is mentioned in My holy word. Myself is the principle of the certainty of Christ."

> *"For they being ignorant of God's righteousness, and seeking to establish their own righteousness, have not submitted to the righteousness of God. For Christ is the end of the law for righteousness to everyone who believes."* Romans 10:3-4

God says, "I know what's best for you. You'll always have to rest and let your pride be destroyed by that fact. I will not always please you in the manner in which you want to be pleased. I'll please you in ways in which I want you to be pleased."

> *"Now I, Nebuchadnezzar, praise and extol and honor the King of heaven, all of whose works are truth, and His ways justice. And those who walk in pride He is able to abase."* Daniel 4:37

February 3

Humility says, "I don't need to have my way. If I let God have His way in me, I don't need my way."

"...Yes, all of you be submissive to one another, and be clothed with humility, for 'God resists the proud, but gives grace to the humble.' Therefore humble yourselves under the mighty hand of God, that He may exalt you in due time." 1 Peter 5:5b-6

God says, "Christ Jesus rejected all the calls of greatness upon His life, yet your earth nature is to try to be great in the eyes of other men. That puts you last before God. To be great before the eyes of God is to be last in the eyes of men. If you will lay down your life for Me, I will raise you up."

"...but whoever desires to become great among you, let him be your servant. And whoever desires to be first among you, let him be your slave—just as the Son of Man did not come to be served, but to serve, and to give His life a ransom for many." Matthew 20:26-28

February 4

God says, "I will love you, forgive you, encourage you, stand with you; but if you step backwards from My way, I'll wait patiently, because who has the time? I do. Who does not have the time to dally and to flit here and there? You!"

> *"And working together with Him, we also urge you not to receive the grace of God in vain—for He says, 'At the acceptable time I listened to you, and on the day of salvation I helped you.' Behold, now is the acceptable time, behold, now is the day of salvation."* 2 Corinthians 6:1-2 (NASB)

God says, "Do not forget My angels are here among you, as well as My Spirit. Give homage, and acknowledge My presence. Give Me joy and give Me thanks and glory for the progress I've made among you that you may grow further and further up the ladder to the eternal Mount Zion upon which Moses found his peace with God before he departed and went to be with Me."

> *"He has shown you, O man, what is good; and what does the Lord require of you but to do justly, to love mercy, and to walk humbly with your God?"* Micah 6:8

February 5

God says, "Don't be indebted to any man in any way—emotionally, financially, or otherwise. You owe your whole life to Christ alone."

"Or what agreement has the temple of God with idols? For we are the temple of the living God; Just as God has said, 'I will dwell in them and walk among them. I will be their God, and they shall be my people.'" 2 Corinthians 6:16 (NASB)

God says, "Prosperity is not in your checkbook. That's so diminutive of you to presume on Me that I want you to have great wealth in the natural world, and all the time you neglected the wealth of the spiritual realm."

"By humility and the fear of the Lord are riches and honor and life." Proverbs 22:4

"But lay up for yourselves treasures in heaven... for where your treasure is, there your heart will be also." Matthew 6:20a, 21

February 6

God says, "What is not of Me is always going to be not of Me, and what is of Me is always going to be of Me. If it's not of Me, it's not in My interest or yours to be involved in that particular mode of activity."

> *"Why do you spend your money for that which is not bread, and your earnings for what does not satisfy? Hearken diligently to Me, and eat what is good, and let your soul delight itself in fatness [the profuseness of spiritual joy]. Incline your ear [submit and consent to the Divine will] and come to Me; hear, and your soul will revive..."* Isaiah 55:2-3 (AMP)

God asks, "Wherever you go, do you take Me with you, or do you leave Me behind?"

Lord, I declare you will be the first thought in my heart each day and the last thought each night. I will be presentable to You in spirit and truth. I am going with Christ Jesus all the way.

> *"If I take the wings of the morning, and dwell in the uttermost parts of the sea, even there Your hand shall lead me, and Your right hand shall hold me."* Psalm 139:9-10

February 7

God says, "It's no excuse not to have time for Me, because you can give time to what you want to give time to; and if you really want to spend time with Me, I do not need to push you, cajole you, urge you, or induce you to do that."

> *"...a certain man gave a great supper and invited many,... but they all with one accord began to make excuses. The first said to him, 'I have bought a piece of ground, and I must go and see it...' and another said, 'I have bought five yoke of oxen, and I am going to test them...' Still another said, 'I have married a wife, and therefore I cannot come.'"* Luke 14:16,18-20

God says, "I permit you to waste your time, but I will that you make My priority yours. My will is My word, and My word is My way."

> *"But seek for (aim at and strive after) first of all His kingdom, and His righteousness (His way of doing and being right), and then all these things taken together will be given you besides."* Matthew 6:33 (AMP)

February 8

God says, "Do not allow the enemy to come against you with one of his very subtle devices that he uses so cleverly against My children to get them to run to and fro and to hurry hither and thither and to be caught up in the business of the world around them."

Are we busy in busyness?

> *"That we should no longer be children, tossed to and fro and carried about with every wind of doctrine, by the trickery of men, in the cunning craftiness by which they lie in wait to deceive..."*
> Ephesians 4:14

God says, "I am always there for you, whether it's in the busy din of your daily rush, at work, or going to and from. I'm always there waiting for you to give Me your attention. That's all I want, My people, is for you to give Me your attention; and I'll make a way through the wilderness of your daily life that you cannot understand."

> *"Receive, please, instruction from His mouth, and lay up His words in your heart."* Job 22:22

February 9

God says, "Whatever you do, remember I am your priority. I must be first, and I will honor what you do, and I will increase your ability to do it."

1. God must be our priority.
2. God's priorities must be ours.
3. God is to be the priority before all things you do; for if He's not in control, you will not be in control.

> *"But what things were gain to me, these I have counted loss for Christ."* Philippians 3:7

God says, "You may seek to have, that you may give, if I am first. You may seek to enlarge your horizons, lengthen your cords, and strengthen your stakes, if I am first. You may seek to be joyful, happy, build the family, build friendships, build your career, if I am first. But My being first means I will lead you into the way you should go. I will lead your every step. My Son was your example. He was led by Me totally. He never said or did anything, except I spoke or showed it to Him beforehand."

> *"My son, give me your heart, and let your eyes observe my ways."* Proverbs 23:26

February 10

God asks, "Do you not know that there's a better way for you than you are walking today? Do you not know there's a better thought for you to think than you thought today? This day can be a day in which I have complete Lordship, and you will know My direction, because you will be comforted by My voice."

> " 'For My thoughts are not your thoughts, nor are your ways My ways,' says the Lord. 'For as the heavens are higher than the earth, so are My ways higher than your ways, and My thoughts than your thoughts.'" Isaiah 55:8-9

God says, "There is a spiritual wholeness that comes from being singularly set upon God, and with your focus being entirely on Me, and your entire priority is Me."

> "The Lord will be awesome to them, for He will reduce to nothing all the gods of the earth; people shall worship Him, each one from his place, indeed all the shores of the nations."
> Zephaniah 2:11

February 11

God says, "If I am not your Lord in a certain area or your King in a certain area, I am not your Lord or your King, but something else or someone else is your lord and king in that area."

"Not every one who says to Me, 'Lord, Lord,' shall enter the kingdom of heaven, but he who does the will of My Father in heaven." Matthew 7:21

God says we should have three things in our lives:

Superiority—Our lives should show the superiority of God.

Preference—Will I obey God or will I obey man?

Preeminence—God should be greater than anything else. He should have the "right of way."

"Whom have I in heaven but You? And I have no delight or desire on earth besides You."
Psalm 73:25 (AMP)

February 12

God says, "Realize you were never born to be yourself. You were born to be Myself. Your flesh must never have priority over My demand upon your daily moments."

> *"Before I formed you in the womb I knew you;*
> *before you were born I sanctified you; and I*
> *ordained you a prophet to the nations." Then*
> *said I: "Ah, Lord God! Behold, I cannot speak,*
> *for I am a youth." But the Lord said to me:*
> *"Do not say, 'I am a youth,' for you shall go to*
> *all to whom I send you, and whatever I*
> *command you, you shall speak."* Jeremiah 1:5-7

The first aim as a believer is to please God.

> *"That you may walk worthy of the Lord, fully*
> *pleasing Him, being fruitful in every good work*
> *and increasing in the knowledge of God."*
> Colossians 1:10

Even Christ said,

> *"...the Father has not left Me alone, for I*
> *always do those things that please Him."*
> John 8:29b

Our aim is to also do those things that always please the Father.

February 13

God says, "Do not let anything but your resolve to please Me be the first priority of your life. And make it clear to others that you are putting God first, no matter what is the cost."

"Finally then, brethren, we request and exhort you in the Lord Jesus, that as you received from us instruction as to how you ought to walk and please God...that you excel still more."
1 Thessalonians 4:1 (NASB)

God says, "Singleness is for one purpose—to learn to be wedded to Christ Jesus. After you are wedded to Christ, He will grant you the desires of your heart."

"I will betroth you to Me forever; Yes, I will betroth you to Me in righteousness and justice, in lovingkindness and mercy." Hosea 2:19

"But I want you to be without care. He who is unmarried cares for the things that belong to the Lord—how he may please the Lord."
1 Corinthians 7:32

February 14

God says, "Put My Son first, is what I want you to do. When you're seeking the kingdom first, you are first with Me. When you're pleasing My Son and the words of life, you please Me, for you've exercised your accountability. You've begun responsibly to respond to My call."

"Strengthen (complete, perfect) and make you what you ought to be and equip you with everything good that you may carry out His will; [while He Himself] works in you and accomplishes that which is pleasing in His sight, through Jesus Christ...." Hebrews 13:21 (AMP)

God asks, "Do you give more allegiance to the world than you do to God? Are you so busy living your life, you don't have time for God?"

"All of you must keep awake (give strict attention, be cautious and active) and watch and pray, that you may not come into temptation. The spirit indeed is willing, but the flesh is weak." Matthew 26:41 (AMP)

February 15

God says, "Your priority should be for Me now, to not just take time to meet and then be spiritual, and then depart and be in the flesh."

"...the Spirit Whom He has caused to dwell in us yearns over us and He yearns for the Spirit [to be welcome] with a jealous love."
James 4:5b (AMP)

God says, "You do not know My awesomeness, or you would never give anything liberty to have priority over you but Me. I not only have a right to have you, you have no right to refuse Me."

"...and you have praised the gods of silver and gold, bronze and iron, wood and stone, which do not see or hear or know; and the God who holds your breath in His hand and owns all your ways, you have not glorified." Daniel 5:23b

February 16

God says, "The nature of God in you is trying to be supreme, but the nature of flesh in you is trying to be supreme, also, so which one will be the priority in your life, My Spirit or your flesh? Will you let your flesh continue to have the majority of the time you have on this earth, or will you let your spirit be free to be in My presence?"

"And he did evil because he did not prepare his heart to seek the Lord." 2 Chronicles 12:14

Settle the war in yourself by the word of God.

God says, "Your flesh will consume most of your earthly life. Your spirit man will consume only bits and tad bits here and there of My precious truths."

"...certainly every man at his best state is but vapor. Selah. Surely every man walks about like a shadow; surely they busy themselves in vain; He heaps up riches, and does not know who will gather them." Psalm 39:5b-6

February 17

God asks, "Are you willing to lay down those things you've been distracted by and that cut Me from coming into your heart? Are you willing to set aside those priorities that you believe are more important than your priority to Me? Are you able to say, 'Yes, Lord, I am willing to be made willing?'"

"Take heed, watch and pray; for you do not know when the time is." Mark 13:33

"... and he said, Lord, I believe! [Constantly] help my weakness of faith!" Mark 9:24b (AMP)

God says, "I perceive that some of you are busy with busyness and idle with spiritualness."

"He who is faithful in what is least is faithful also in much; and he who is unjust in what is least is unjust also in much." Luke 16:10

"I have chosen the way of truth and faithfulness; Your ordinances have I set before me."
Psalm 119:30 (AMP)

February 18

God says, "Too many of My children are having done with the greater things (of God). They are majoring in the minors, and they're minoring in the majors. Their priorities are not straight."

Love God enough to be spirit men. Love Him enough to have done with lesser things.

> *"Therefore I say to you, do not worry about your life, what you will eat or what you will drink..."*
> Matthew 6:25

God has given specific guidelines to ordering our priorities throughout the day. He says to:

1. Have done with lesser things.
2. Do the necessary things.
3. Always return to your first love.

Lesser things are all those things that distract us from seeking God's presence. Necessary things are to be kept at a minimum.

> *"But I have this [one charge to make] against you: that you have left (abandoned) the love you had at first...Remember then from what heights you have fallen. Repent...and do the works you did previously [when first you knew the Lord]..."*
> Revelation 2:4-5a (AMP)

February 19

God says, "Look up, for your redemption draws nigh, and I am here, even at the door of your heart knocking; but only you can open the heart door and let Me in this day."

"Then you will seek Me, inquire for, and require Me [as a vital necessity] and find Me when you search for Me with all your heart."
Jeremiah 29:13 (AMP)

We are to ask God to open the eyes of our hearts. Lord, we want to see You.

"[For I always pray to] the God of our Lord Jesus Christ, the Father of Glory, that He may grant you a spirit of wisdom and revelation [of insight into mysteries and secrets] in the [deep and intimate] knowledge of Him, by having the eyes of your heart flooded with light..."
Ephesians 1:17-18b (AMP)

February 20

God says, "If you seek Me early, you will find Me. I'll be in the dawn air when you wake, and when you go to sleep, I'll be there with My angels around you, and you shall see that I am your God and Jehovah."

"I love those who love Me, and those who seek Me early and diligently shall find Me."
Proverbs 8:17 (AMP)

God says, "I'm pleased with My people who desire Me with all their hearts. I'm pleased to see, even though the world would mock you, that you want to go all the way with Me, across every desert, go through every valley, across the wildest storms of the sea, to find your harbor of safety in My garden of truth."

"...the Lord has proclaimed you to be His special people, just as He has promised you, that you should keep all His commandments, and that He will set you high above all nations which He has made, in praise, in name, and in honor, and that you may be a holy people to the Lord your God, just as He has spoken."
Deuteronomy 26:18-19

February 21

God says, "My Son is the Truth giver. He is the Truth standard. He is the bearer of the sword of the Spirit. In His word, which He executes, is love, and life, and health for you. He will touch you, today, if you will allow Him. He will touch you wherever you need, but you must want Him more than you want life."

"Not that we are sufficient of ourselves to think of anything as being from ourselves, but our sufficiency is from God." 2 Corinthians 3:5

God says, "If you seek My ways, you must bend your ways to Mine. You must allow yourself to be denied, that you might give credence to your God."

"For the grace of God that brings salvation has appeared to all men, teaching us that, denying ungodliness and worldly lusts, we should live soberly, righteously, and godly in the present age." Titus 2:11-12

February 22

God says, "Keep your eyes on Me, your spiritual eyes. Your natural eyes cannot see Me clearly or understand Me."

*"I know that You can do everything, and that
no purpose of Yours can be withheld from You.
I have heard of You by the hearing of the ear,
but now my eye sees You."* Job 42:2,5

God says, "One of the greatest achievements you can ever have in this life is to learn to be comfortable alone with God."

We need to learn to practice the presence of God.

*"One thing I have desired of the Lord, that will
I seek; that I may dwell in the house of the Lord
all the days of my life, to behold the beauty of
the Lord, and to inquire in His temple."*
Psalm 27:4

February 23

God says, "Seek your rest. Seek to rise. Seek to think the best. Seek joy in the midst of trial. And above all, seek Me."

"Seek the Lord [...require Him as the foremost necessity of your life], all you humble of the land who have acted in compliance with His revealed will and have kept His commandments; seek righteousness, seek humility.... It may be you will be hidden in the day of the Lord's anger."
Zephaniah 2:3 (AMP)

God says, "The spirit life is what you are to seek first. The kingdom of God is a spirit life. My Spirit seeks spirits of like kind and quality, birthed by the new birth, immersed in Him and manifesting the spirit life."

"For the kingdom of God is not eating and drinking, but righteousness and peace and joy in the Holy Spirit." Romans 14:17

"Seek the Lord and His strength;
Seek His face forevermore!" Psalm 105:4

February 24

God says, "Do not plead for things your flesh yearns for, but seek first God's kingdom and His righteousness." (See Matthew 6:33.)

God says, "Plead not for the things that your flesh yearns for, and that you ache for in your soul. For I have priorities—the kingdom of God and His righteousness. And what placates your soul at this time will not placate your spirit, but that which placates your spirit and edifies and exalts the name of Jesus in your spirit will also edify your flesh."

God says, "It behooves you now to get serious with Me. For the first time in your life, realize your very existence at the next minute from now depends on Me. Without Me, your heart could fail. Your very life could fail."

"In whose hand is the life of every living thing, and the breath of all mankind?" Job 12:10

February 25

God says, "By an act of your will, you have to open the door, that the glory of God may come in your life, that you may change all perspectives in your mind and spirit and heart, that He might begin to show you the lengthening of your days in spirit and in truth."

"Behold, I stand at the door and knock. If anyone hears My voice and opens the door, I will come in to him and dine with him, and he with Me." Revelation 3:20

God asks, "Are you daily seeking the Lord who you are going to be married to forever?"

"For I am zealous for you with a godly eagerness and a divine jealousy, for I have betrothed you to one Husband, to present you as a chaste virgin to Christ." 2 Corinthians 11:2 (AMP)

February 26

God says, "I'm always there to comfort, to love, to lift up, to edify you; but you must do it My way. You must want My way. You must want it above what you want in your mind, in your emotions, in your will. You must want Me more than life itself, for I am your only life. I'm the only life you'll find ten thousand years from now."

"As the deer pants for the water brooks, so pants my soul for You, O God. My soul thirsts for God, for the living God. When shall I come and appear before God?" Psalm 42:1-2

God says, "I want you to know if any man will seek Me, search for Me, he will find Me when he does so with all his heart, soul, mind, and strength. You must not want what I do not want for you. You must not seek what I do not want you to have. You must not labor in that whereunto you're not called to labor."

"...God said, 'I have found David... a man after My own heart, who will do all My will.'"
Acts 13:22b

February 27

God says, "Take time to be alone and to sit and to seek Me with your whole heart, and you will find Me. I do not reveal Myself to those with the degree that I want to who are not totally sold out to Me."

"And it shall be to him and his descendents after him a covenant of an everlasting priesthood, because he was zealous for his God, and made atonement for the children of Israel."
Numbers 25:13

God says, "There is no reason why all men cannot seek Me. There is no reason why all truth seekers should not be pressing into the kingdom tonight."

"I will run in the way of Your commandments, for You shall enlarge my heart." Psalm 119:32

"For the eyes of the Lord run to and fro throughout the whole earth, to show Himself strong on behalf of those whose heart is loyal to Him...." 2 Chronicles 16:9a

February 28

God says, "There are things I would have you do that you are not doing. There are things I would have you say that you are not saying. There are things I would have you pray that you are not praying; so come away, My beloved, and seek My peace."

"Then Jesus answered and said to them, 'Most assuredly, I say to you, the Son can do nothing of Himself, but what He sees the Father do; for whatever He does, the Son also does in like manner.'" John 5:19

God says, "My children are looking too much to 'all these things shall be added' and not enough to 'seek first.'"

"But seek first the kingdom of God and His righteousness, and all these things shall be added to you." Matthew 6:33

"And whatever you do, do it heartily as to the Lord and not to men, knowing that from the Lord you will receive the reward of the inheritance; for you serve the Lord Christ." Colossians 3:23-24

February 29

Correct yourself so that God can correct you.

*"Our iniquities, our secret heart and its sins
[which we would so like to conceal even from
ourselves], You have set in the [revealing] light
of Your countenance."* Psalm 90:8 (AMP)

God says, "If you seriously want to get to the source of a problem, there's only one place to go. You need to look no further than your own heart."

*"Then I will give them one heart, and I will put
a new spirit within them, and take the stony
heart out of their flesh, and give them a heart
of flesh."* Ezekiel 11:19

God says, "Repent of those times I have tried to cut things from your life, those times when I have tried to tell you with gentle words, things you should do to make yourself more like Me. Repent of that, My children, today."

March 1

God says, "Believer, let all lying cease!"

"Therefore, putting away lying, 'Let each one of you speak truth with his neighbor,' for we are members of one another." Ephesians 4:25

"Let the lying lips be put to silence..."
Psalm 31:18a

The believer must commit to being completely open and transparent before his God!

God says, "Do not react to what I say. React to what you've done. React to your heart."

"The sacrifices of God are a broken spirit, a broken and a contrite heart—these, O God, you will not despise." Psalm 51:17

March 2

God says, "Come before My altar. Weep and bow and cry out, and go away with a new heart and a right spirit... for behold, today is the day when all things are done to please My will."

"Create in me a clean heart, O God, and renew a steadfast spirit within me. Restore to me the joy of Your salvation, and uphold me by Your generous spirit." Psalm 51:10,12

God says, "You can please Me by remembering to repent daily. The fruits of repentance are meekness, a humble heart, contrite spirit, and gentleness to My correction, a gentleness to My chastisement, a gentleness to My scourging."

God asks, "Are you freely able to receive My correction and not wither, not run, not be afraid, not protest, and not be angry? Then you are free to rise, to rise high and never come back to former days."

March 3

God says, "Until true repentance comes, there will be no peace, because true repentance is complete change, one hundred eighty degrees from the wrong to the right. True repentance is from a heart that says...I will not offend God."

"Bear fruits that are deserving and consistent with [your] repentance [that is, conduct worthy of a heart changed, a heart abhorring sin]..."
Luke 3:8a (AMP)

God says, "Be reconciled to Me before you are reconciled to another."

"That is, that God was in Christ reconciling the world to Himself, not imputing their trespasses to them, and has committed to us the word of reconciliation. Now then, we are ambassadors for Christ, as though God were pleading through us: we implore you on Christ's behalf, be reconciled to God." 2 Corinthians 5:19-20

March 4

God says, "Knowing the truth of My word is the traditional approach to My nature and My ways. You are to know Me in spirit and truth. Spirit only can understand spiritual truth. Flesh cannot teach spirit, for flesh profits nothing (See John 6:63.) How to disengage the mind is the dilemma you face. Let mental exercise cease, and let spirit take charge."

> *"For it is written: 'I will destroy the wisdom of the wise, and bring to nothing the understanding of the prudent.'"* 1 Corinthians 1:19

God says, "I offer you Myself and My unlimited resources of the Spirit who created all the universe around you, who will do what He says when you have come in spirit to the measure of the truth you have already learned. It's My Spirit which shall give you the ability to go beyond measure..."

> *"For since He Whom God has sent speaks the words of God... God does not give Him His Spirit sparingly or by measure, but boundless is the gift God makes of His Spirit!"* John 3:34 (AMP)

March 5

God says, "If you have a willing spirit, it means you have an affinity and a bonding to My Spirit, and that means that words of truth can come into your spirit mightily, and you can overcome the imperfections, if you grow stronger in the Spirit."

> *"But now you also must complete the doing of it; that as there was a readiness to desire it, so there also may be a completion out of what you have."* 2 Corinthians 8:11

God says, "I'm not going to concern Myself with what is not spirit and truth. That's available in plenteous amounts in this earth. You can go anywhere you want to and find out what is not spirit and truth, and discover it all around you. It's meant to engage the body and mind in the law of sin and death."

> *"For those who live according to the flesh set their minds on the things of the flesh, but those who live according to the Spirit, the things of the Spirit. For to be carnally minded is death, but to be spiritually minded is life and peace."*
> Romans 8:5-6

March 6

God says, "If you lived, and moved, and had your being in the central truth that justice is in you, the Justifier is in you, and the One who exalts the spirit and truth is in you, that is your hope of glory."

> *"For in Him the whole fullness of Deity (the Godhead) continues to dwell in bodily form [giving complete expression of the divine nature]. And you are in Him, made full and having come to fullness of life [in Christ you too are filled with the Godhead—Father, Son and Holy Spirit—and reach full spiritual stature]. And He is the Head of all rule and authority [of every angelic principality and power]."* Colossians 2:9-10 (AMP)

God says, "Reconciliation is reconciling that which is part spirit and part flesh for all spirit and that which is part truth for all truth."

> *"Now all things are of God, who has reconciled us to Himself through Jesus Christ, and has given us the ministry of reconciliation."*
>
> 2 Corinthians 5:18

March 7

When you don't mention the name of Christ to the unbelieving world, you can be sure they will not mention Him.

Start today by examining yourself whether you be in the faith.

"Then I said, 'I will not make mention of Him, nor speak anymore in His name.' But His word was in my heart like a burning fire shut up in my bones; I was weary of holding it back, and I could not." Jeremiah 20:9

God says, "Someone must speak for God. That someone is you, if you've been taught the truth. Now execute My word. Execute My word with the faith of God, for you are My voices in this land."

"Since we have such [glorious] hope (such joyful and confident expectation), we speak very freely and openly and fearlessly." 2 Corinthians 3:12 (AMP)

"And daily in the temple, and in every house, they did not cease teaching and preaching Jesus as the Christ." Acts 5:42

March 8

God asks, "Are you aloof from every need of being a light in this world? When were you a light in this world? When last did you become a pillar of light to others who had never seen the light of Christ?"

"Let your light so shine before men that they may see your moral excellence and your praise-worthy, noble, and good deeds and recognize and honor and praise and glorify your Father Who is in heaven." Matthew 5:16 (AMP)

God says, "But I have come to seek those who are lost, to restore those who are blind, and to give sight to those who do not have spiritual vision."

"The Spirit of the Lord is upon Me, because He has anointed Me to preach the gospel to the poor; He has sent Me to heal the broken-hearted, to proclaim liberty to the captives and recovery of sight to the blind, to set at liberty those who are oppressed." Luke 4:18

March 9

God asks, "'Who will go for Me?' But My people hesitate. They wait. They always wait for someone else to go. If I say you can go, you can go. The greatest work I gave you, and the reason you are filled with the Spirit, is to go out in the world and be a witness for Me."

"He saw that there was no man, and wondered that there was no intercessor; therefore His own arm brought salvation for Him; and His own righteousness, it sustained Him."
Isaiah 59:16

God says, "People are perishing because you've not said anything. Speak words of life to people, not words of death. Speak hope. Do not speak pessimistically, because you should be supremely confident because you're in Me, and I'm in you."

"Death and life are in the power of the tongue, and those who love it will eat its fruit."
Proverbs 18:21

"And my tongue shall speak of Your righteousness and of Your praise all the day long."
Psalm 35:28

March 10

God says, "Anticipate meeting those who will be sent to you by God, and recognize that when people cross your path, they might be sent by God for you to love, and forgive, and to restore."

"And those who turn many to righteousness shall shine like the stars forever and ever."
Daniel 12:3

"So we are Christ's ambassadors, God making His appeal as it were through us. We [as Christ's personal representatives] beg you for His sake to lay hold of the divine favor [now offered you] and be reconciled to God."
2 Corinthians 5:20 (AMP)

God says, "Even the stranger you meet will know later that they've met a child of God. Be unafraid, for God made you to be a bright light for others, weary travelers on the road to life, that you may speak, and they will hear. Grab somebody with love and restore them through the Son of God."

(Christ said) "For I was hungry and you gave Me food; I was thirsty and you gave Me drink; I was a stranger and you took Me in."
Matthew 25:35

March 11

God says, "Defend Me, I say. Defend Me from even your own family. Defend Me from even your own friends. Defend Me from even your own self."

"But none of these things move me; nor do I count my life dear to myself, so that I may finish my race with joy, and the ministry which I received from the Lord Jesus, to testify to the gospel of the grace of God. For I have not shunned to declare to you the whole counsel of God." Acts 20:24,27

God says, "Be ambassadors. Do not be ashamed of Me, because if you're ashamed of Me in this age, I will be ashamed of you when you appear before Me with the angels. So do not be ashamed. Speak forth, plant your feet and let people know who you are. They will be astonished that there are people like you on this earth."

"For whoever is ashamed of Me and My words in this adulterous and sinful generation, of him the Son of Man also will be ashamed when He comes in the glory of His Father with the holy angels." Mark 8:38

March 12

God says, "You cannot love someone if you don't warn them. I said speak the truth in love; and when you warn the wicked of their way, and they repent, then you have saved a soul. But if you do not warn them, their blood will be on your hands."

"...and if you do not speak to warn the wicked from his way, that wicked man shall die in his iniquity; but his blood I will require at your hand. Nevertheless if you warn the wicked to turn from his way, and he does not turn from his way, he shall die in his iniquity; but you have delivered your soul." Ezekiel 33:8-9

God says, "Learn to praise Me now. Learn to love Me now. Learn to meditate in Me now. Learn to tell the people what God's done in your life, for God is a mighty one who heals you, who sets you free, who lifts you up and causes you to be glorified in His name. For the glory of God shall fall upon My people."

"For you will be His witness to all men of what you have seen and heard." Acts 22:15

March 13

Your strongest testimony for Christ is your daily life. When you begin to witness for Christ, the people will listen and believe because they can see Christ in your life.

> *"And have clothed yourself with the new [spiritual self], which is [ever in the process of being] renewed and remolded into [fuller and more perfect knowledge upon] knowledge after the image (the likeness) of Him Who created it."*
>
> Colossians 3:10 (AMP)

God says, "I will not accuse you. The words you speak, the life you live, and the fruit you bear will be your accuser or your witness for the life you lived for Me."

> *"Every branch in Me that does not bear fruit He takes away; and every branch that bears fruit He prunes, that it may bear more fruit."*
>
> John 15:2

March 14

God says, "The goal is for the Christ nature to be totally seen by the world to be in you; and when people see and hear and dwell on you, they will think only of the fact that God has got a hold of you."

"By which have been given to us exceedingly great and precious promises, that through these you may be partakers of the divine nature, having escaped the corruption that is in the world through lust." 2 Peter 1:4

God says, "You must open your mouth and reveal your spirit, and not reveal your flesh, for I abhor flesh."

"If anyone speaks, let him speak as the oracles of God..." 1 Peter 4:11a

"Listen, for I will speak of excellent things, and from the opening of my lips will come right things; for my mouth will speak truth... all the words of my mouth are with righteousness; nothing crooked or perverse is in them."
Proverbs 8:6,7a,8

March 15

God says, "Before you have interaction with each other, you are to prepare yourselves to be the essence of Christ and speak as the Holy Spirit would speak."

> *"For we are the sweet fragrance of Christ [which exhales] unto God..."* 2 Corinthians 2:15a (AMP)

> *"Let your speech always be with grace, seasoned with salt, that you may know how you ought to answer each one."* Colossians 4:6

God says, "Remember, My Son did not even allow Himself as God in flesh, to teach His disciples. Because He was discipled by Me in His earthly body, He did nothing and said nothing except as it was given Him by His Father."

> *"Do you not believe that I am in the Father, and the Father in Me? The words that I speak to you I do not speak on My own authority; but the Father who dwells in Me does the works."*
> John 14:10

> *"For I have not spoken on My own authority; but the Father who sent Me gave Me a command, what I should say and what I should speak."* John 12:49

March 16

God says, "Don't talk much to men of those things which you have spoken little about to God."

"My mouth shall tell of Your righteous acts and of Your deeds of salvation all the day..."
Psalm 71:15a (AMP)

"...for out of the abundance of the heart the mouth speaks....for every idle word men may speak, they will give account of it in the day of judgment. For by your words you will be justified, and by your words you will be condemned."
Matthew 12:34b,36b-37

God asks, "Are you exercising your lordship, kingship, and priestly role in administering the word, the work, and the life of the Lord?"

"And as you go, preach, saying, 'The kingdom of heaven is at hand.' Heal the sick, cleanse the lepers, raise the dead, cast out demons. Freely you have received, freely give." Matthew 10:7-8

"Therefore settle it in your hearts not to meditate beforehand on what you will answer; for I will give you a mouth and wisdom which all your adversaries will not be able to contradict or resist." Luke 21:14-15

March 17

God says, "Let your conversation be sprinkled with the salt of My Spirit. Talk and speak gently. Have your conversation filled with the lovely things of God. Let the love of Christ exude itself from the pores of your very bodies. Let everything you do give Me honor and glory."

"Let no corrupt communication proceed out of your mouth, but what is good for necessary edification." Ephesians 4:29

God says, "Let not corrupt communication proceed from your mouth, but that which is for edification. Let your yea be yea and your nay be nay. Better that you would not speak than to speak those things of darkness; for out of the abundance of the heart a man speaks."

"...I have purposed that my mouth shall not transgress." Psalm 17:3

"I said, 'I will guard my ways, lest I sin with my tongue; I will restrain my mouth with a muzzle...'" Psalm 39:1

March 18

God says, "Leave the understanding of spiritual principles up to Me to fix in the heart of men. That's a God purpose. I place the word in such a way that the prince of darkness cannot steal it."

*"He has made everything beautiful in its time.
Also He has put eternity in their hearts...I know
that whatever God does, it shall be forever.
Nothing can be added to it, and nothing taken
from it. God does it, that men should fear before
Him."* Ecclesiastes 3:11,14

God says, "It's distressing to you that you are laboring in the harvest field, and there's no harvest from that individual. But it should not be surprising to you. My Son labored for years among you on this earth as God in flesh, and never had harmony at any time, never had unity, never had a complete understanding and bond between all twelve."

*"But you shall hold fast to the Lord your God,
as you have done to this day."* Joshua 23:8

March 19

God says, "When you find the reality of your spirit walk, death has gone into a lost and totally defeated grave."

"But when this perishable will have put on the imperishable, and this mortal will have put on immortality, then will come about the saying that is written: 'Death is swallowed up in victory. O death, where is your victory? O death, where is your sting?'" 1 Corinthians 15:54-55 (NASB)

God says, "Just as your lives are a cyclic walk from glory to glory, from one level of existence to another, as you seek to be spiritual and be led of Me and My truth, realize that I will make everything new. Do not be afraid of change, for with it comes responsibility in My kingdom; and if you are faithful in those things I've given you, I will make you responsible in more things."

"His Lord said to him, 'Well done, good and faithful servant; you were faithful over a few things, I will make you ruler over many things. Enter into the joy of your Lord.'" Matthew 25:21

March 20

Being in the Spirit doesn't mean you're in charge; it means God's in charge in you.

> *"Let be and be still, and know [recognize and understand] that I am God. I will be exalted among the nations! I will be exalted in the earth!"* Psalm 46:10 (AMP)

The enemy's intention is to make us an enemy of ourselves.

God says, "Try to climb a mountain that is sheer ice with your bare hands, with your flesh. You cannot do it. You have a mountain to climb in the spirit realm, but you can soar in the spirit. The spirit has no problem and does not need the flesh to walk. The spirit just rises because it has been trained to follow My Shepherd, My Son Jesus."

> *"But you, beloved, build yourselves up [founded] on your most holy faith [make progress, rise like an edifice higher and higher], praying in the Holy Spirit."* Jude 20 (AMP)

> *"Now when they came up out of the water, the Spirit of the Lord caught Philip away..."* Acts 8:39

March 21

God says, "The promised land is where My people dwell in perfect peace and harmony with My word and Spirit and spiritual principles, and My tranquility is controlling you at all times, and you're always in charge of your emotional nature. You're always in charge of your tendencies to see the darkness and see the evil."

"Therefore, since a promise remains of entering His rest, let us fear lest any of you seem to have come short of it." Hebrews 4:1

God says, "You will find that as you journey upward and into the spiritual realm, that My demands will seem to be more ruthless upon you and more like that of a taskmaster."

Moses struck the rock in anger, rather than speak to it to bring water forth as God commanded him, and he was not allowed to enter the promised land.

"Because you trespassed against Me...because you did not hallow Me in the midst of the children of Israel." Deuteronomy 32:51

March 22

God says, "When you're active in the flesh realm, you cannot be active in the spiritual realm."

"I say then: Walk in the Spirit, and you shall not fulfill the lust of the flesh. For the flesh lusts against the Spirit, and the Spirit against the flesh; and these are contrary to one another, so that you do not do the things that you wish."
Galatians 5:16-17

God says, "I invite you to come in, but don't come in to come out, but come in to stay."

"Come to Me, all you who labor and are heavy laden, and I will give you rest. Take My yoke upon you and learn from Me, for I am gentle and lowly in heart, and you will find rest for your souls." Matthew 11:28-29

March 23

God says, "Sow in the spiritual realm if you're going to harvest in the physical realm...the spiritual man will always lead the natural man into a land of plenty."

"Who will transform our lowly body that it may be conformed to His glorious body, according to the working by which He is able even to subdue all things to Himself." Philippians 3:21

God says, "The language of the Spirit is that which is a conveyor belt for you to travel upon rather swiftly. Learn the secret of releasing the Spirit word, the Spirit language, the Spirit life."

"What is the conclusion then? I will pray with the spirit, and I will also pray with the understanding. I will sing with the spirit, and I will also sing with the understanding."
1 Corinthians 14:15-16

March 24

God says, "Spiritual pleasure is when I reveal Myself to the human spirit. When you are not fascinated, you are vulnerable. Being fascinated is having a wondering spirit."

Say, "I love to love you, Lord."

> *"Blessed is the man whom You choose, and cause to approach You, that he may dwell in Your courts. We shall be satisfied with the goodness of Your house, of Your holy temple."*
> Psalm 65:4

God says, "Rejoice that there is such a wonderful adventure for you no matter what happens in the natural world around you or in you. You will still have this spiritual adventure, which is the only joy you will really have in this life."

> *(Christ prayed) "...I say these things while I am still in the world, so that My joy may be made full and complete and perfect in them [that they may experience My delight fulfilled in them, that My enjoyment may be perfected in their own souls, that they may have My gladness within them, filling their hearts]."* John 17:13 (AMP)

March 25

God says, "The principle of eternity is the principle of Christ. The principle of Christ is the principle of life. The principle of life is the principle of truth, and the principle of truth is the principle of the Spirit; and Spirit is God, and God is Spirit, and the Son and the Holy Spirit and I are one."

"He who has the Son has life; He who does not have the Son of God does not have life."
1 John 5:12

God says, "In My kingdom you shall find that you are without the fear of the enemy, for the enemy will not reign and rule in My holy place. There will be no evil, no disease, no sin, no sickness, no sorrow, no anxiety, no fear. There will be an anticipation each moment of your existence that there is a rapturous life to live that passes the significance of this human life. My kingdom begins on this earth, but it continues into eternity."

"And God will wipe away every tear from their eyes; there shall be no more death, nor sorrow, nor crying; and there shall be no more pain, for the former things have passed away." Revelation 21:4

March 26

God can cause you to come along with Him, but He says it's far better if you come willingly, frequently, and hungrily.

"When You said, 'Seek My face,' my heart said to You, 'Your face, Lord, I will seek.'" Psalm 27:8

"Oh, send out Your light and Your truth! Let them lead me..." Psalm 43:3a

God says, "Maturity of the spirit is when you invite God to be Lord over the things you don't want to surrender."

"...let everyone who names [himself by] the name of the Lord give up all iniquity and stand aloof from it." 2 Timothy 2:19b (AMP)

March 27

God says, "I give you permission; but I would love for you to not use your free will but use your spiritual will."

"He went a little farther and fell on His face, and prayed, saying, 'O My Father, if it is possible, let this cup pass from Me; nevertheless, not as I will, but as You will.'" Matthew 26:39

God says, "Take a stand for Me tonight by taking a stand down from your own throne of confidence. Get down off and let Me be Lord. Submit to Me, and I will heal you."

"O Lord my God, I cried out to You, and You healed me." Psalm 30:2

"I said, Lord, be merciful and gracious to me; heal my inner self, for I have sinned against You." Psalm 41:4 (AMP)

March 28

God says, "My children, give up everything you value that is not of Me. Give it up today, and you will be rewarded by blessings that you will not be able to imagine."

"...eye has not seen, nor ear heard, nor have entered into the heart of man the things God has prepared for those who love Him."
1 Corinthians 2:9

God says, "Forsake all that is yours and partake of all that is Mine to give you. Reach out and partake of Me, My life, My Spirit, My love. Give Me homage, praise, and grace, for I have given you all. What more can you give Me that you have withheld? What are you withholding today that could be Mine, I, the King of eternity?"

"Then Jesus said to His disciples, 'If anyone desires to come after Me, let him deny himself, and take up his cross, and follow Me.'"
Matthew 16:24

March 29

God says, "You must be willing to let everything be broken that has been put on the altar of expediency. Let everything be broken. Expect nothing of this world's gain. Expect only the riches of Christ. Expect it and prepare to be recipients of it."

"Command those who are rich in this present age not to be haughty, nor to trust in uncertain riches but in the living God, who gives us richly all things to enjoy." 1 Timothy 6:17

God says, "Jesus Christ is ready and willing. Are you ready? He is able. Are you able? He is calling you today. He wants to loose your bonds and let you follow Him. Come up and see the spring coming, the summer of God's love."

"That nature (creation) itself will be set free from its bondage to decay and corruption [and gain an entrance] into the glorious freedom of God's children." Romans 8:21 (AMP)

"...for when I am weak [in human strength], then am I [truly] strong (able, powerful in divine strength)." 2 Corinthians 12:10 (AMP)

March 30

God says, "If one is fully submissive, and willing, and yielded, and bonded to My ways by submitting to My word and doing it, he or she is under a spiritual principle of protection that will spare them from the injustices of Satan's ways in this world around you."

"The Lord shall preserve you from all evil; He shall preserve your soul. The Lord shall preserve your going out and your coming in from this time forth, and even forevermore." Psalm 121:7-8

God says, "Your full dependency on Me is absolutely essential for any gains to be done in the *huios* maturity God wants. It's worth more than the sacrifice of laying down all that you think is important. I can make you be all that I can make you to be."

"Let us hear the conclusion of the whole matter: Fear God and keep His commandments, for this is the whole duty of man." Ecclesiastes 12:13

March 31

God says, "My Holy Spirit is even now convicting, but they must be willing to say, 'I have determined I will do it the Lord's way.' And then they will be delivered, and it will be well with your soul, saith the Lord."

"I delight to do Your will, O my God: yes, Your law is withing my heart." Psalm 40:8 (AMP)

Will to be a part of truthseeking.

Will to listen to God's word eagerly.

Will to read God's word.

Will to hear God's word.

Go on with an urgency that the time is short.

Count it a time to prepare for what is ahead.

April 1

God says, "I am a Gideonite lover; for I love those who are willing to take what little they have and give it unselfishly to Me. As long as you hold back your time, your efforts, whatever, you are actually dictating to Me what your life shall be. And so, consequently, I cannot intervene against your will."

> *"For the ways of man are directly before the eyes of the Lord, and He [Who would have us live soberly, chastely, and godly] carefully weighs all man's goings."* Proverbs 5:21 (AMP)

> *"There is a way which seems right to a man and appears straight before him, but at the end of it is the way of death."* Proverbs 14:12 (AMP)

God never looks for able people, but for available people.

> *"Also I heard the voice of the Lord, saying: 'Whom shall I send, and who will go for Us?' Then I said, 'Here am I! Send me.'"* Isaiah 6:8

April 2

God says, "Do not make excuses for your walk. Either you're walking with Me, or you're not. You have one master or another, but you can't have two. I'm the Lord God who holds you in His hands; and every heart beat you have is by My permission."

> *"Who among all these does not know that the hand of the Lord has done this, in whose hand is the life of every living thing, and the breath of all mankind?"* Job 12:9-10

God asks, "Will you be willing to submit to Me your very life if I asked for it? That does not mean I will take it; but are you willing to submit it to Me? What life have you apart from Me?"

> *"I have been crucified with Christ; it is no longer I who live, but Christ lives in me; and the life which I now live in the flesh I live by faith in the Son of God, who loved me and gave Himself for me."* Galatians 2:20

April 3

God asks, "When have you last denied yourself the things that have you in trouble in your body and mind? When have you last said, 'No,' for the final time and meant it?"

> *"Remove falsehood and lies far from me; give me neither poverty nor riches—feed me with the food allotted to me; lest I be full and deny You, and say, 'Who is the Lord?' or lest I be poor and steal, and profane the name of my God."*
> Proverbs 30:8-9

God says, "If you can see the prosperity of your soul, you will find health in spirit, mind, body, and finances. The end result is to give them to Me for My caretakership and not your stewardship."

> *"For what is a man profited if he gains the whole world, and loses his own soul? Or what will a man give in exchange for his soul?"*
> Matthew 16:26

> *"...you shall love the Lord your God with all your heart, with all your soul, and with all your mind."* Matthew 22:37

April 4

God says, "To walk as a giant in the spiritual realm is to be willing to die for Me—to die daily, moment by moment, to the circumstances that tempt you to go the way of the world."

> *"And those who are Christ's have crucified the flesh with its passions and desires. If we live in the Spirit, let us also walk in the Spirit."*
> Galatians 5:24-25

God says we can do all things through Christ who strengthens us. We are well able to take the land—the land of stubbornness, pride, resistance, walled cities, and the like.

If God says it, we can do it.

> *"Then Caleb quieted the people before Moses, and said, 'Let us go up at once and take possession, for we are well able to overcome it.'"*
> Numbers 13:30

April 5

God says, "Behold, I do a new thing. I make all things new that are fully surrendered to Me, including your mind and body. Rededicate your mind and body every day of your life, for there the hedge of protection comes down so easily that Satan has a right to come in at will."

"Although my house is not so with God, yet He has made with me an everlasting covenant, ordered in all things and secure. For this is all my salvation and all my desire; Will He not make it increase?" 2 Samuel 23:5

God says, "The clock is your enemy. Spirit does not need time. Spirit only needs willingness. If you're willing, I'll make you to eat of the fat of the land."

God says, "It is possible, My sons, to be perfected instantly."

"Now a certain man was there who had an infirmity thirty-eight years. When Jesus saw him lying there... He said to him, 'Do you want to be made well?'...'Rise, take up your bed and walk.' And immediately the man was made well..." John 5:5-6, 8-9a

April 6

God says, "Even when My children turn their backs on Me, I have to love."

On a daily basis; give yourself to God and treat yourself as if God owned you.

> *"Knowing that you were not redeemed with corruptible things, like silver or gold, from your aimless conduct received by tradition from your fathers, but with the precious blood of Christ, as of a lamb without blemish and without spot."*
> 1 Peter 1:18-19

God says, "Allow Me not to be frustrated by your organization of this or that or the other. Allow Me to do the work."

> *"Trust in the Lord with all your heart, and lean not on your own understanding; in all your ways acknowledge Him, and He shall direct your paths."* Proverbs 3:5-6

April 7

God says, "I'm waiting for My prodigal to come home. If he will but surrender all his self to Me, I will take his self and give him My self. I will take his ways and give him My ways. I will take his stubbornness and give him My willingness, for I am the Lord God. Just have the will to come back to your Father's home."

> *"...but when he came to himself, he said...'I will arise and go to my father, and will say to him, "Father, I have sinned against heaven and before you"' ... "For this my son was dead and is alive again; he was lost and is found..."*
> Luke 15:17-18, 24

God says, "If you're going to have dominion authority over all creation, you're going to have to have dominion over yourself. You need to discipline yourself."

> *"...shall we not much more readily be in subjection to the Father of spirits and live?"*
> Hebrews 12:9b

April 8

When God sees something defiled, He does not hate it. He says, "I love its restoration; I love that which I see will be restored."

"Through the Lord's mercies we are not consumed, because His compassions fail not. They are new every morning; great is Your faithfulness." Lamentations 3:22-23

God says, "Come back, My sons and daughters who have strayed. I love you. I want to perfect that in you. I want to heal you. I want to cleanse you. Let Me do it."

"...bring My sons from afar, and My daughters from the ends of the earth—everyone who is called by My name, whom I have created for My glory; I have formed him, yes, I have made him." Isaiah 43:6b-7

April 9

God says, "Put all things that are not of Me out of your life now by your own effort, your own decision, and your own will. Cleanse your homes. Cleanse your minds. Cleanse your spirits. Cleanse your hearts; for I will deal with the people that seek Me with all their heart, mind, soul, and strength."

> *"Therefore, since these [great] promises are ours, beloved, let us cleanse ourselves from everything that contaminates and defiles body and spirit, and bring [our] consecration to completeness in the [reverential] fear of God."*
> 2 Corinthians 7:1 (AMP)

God says, "Sanctification is the process of yielding to the clean thing and resisting evil. I am doing a new thing in everyone who is progressing toward that mark of the high calling."

> *"And such were some of you. But you were washed, but you were sanctified, but you were justified in the name of the Lord Jesus and by the Spirit of our God."* 1 Corinthians 6:11

April 10

God says, "I am doing a new thing today. I am doing a new thing in each of you that give Me your heart...I will cleanse the vessel that offers himself or herself to Me. I will cleanse them thoroughly and cleanly and perfectly."

"Have mercy upon me, O God, according to Your lovingkindness; according to the multitude of Your tender mercies, blot out my transgressions. Wash me thoroughly from my iniquity, and cleanse me from my sin." Psalm 51:1-2

God says, "Don't forget I'm the deliverer, you're not. I'm the cleanser, you're not. I'm the justifier, you're not. I'm the One who chooses, and you do not choose."

"But of Him you are in Christ Jesus, who became for us wisdom from God—and righteousness and sanctification and redemption—that, as it is written, 'He who glories, let him glory in the Lord.'" 1 Corinthians 1:30-31

"You did not choose Me, but I chose you and appointed you that you should go and bear fruit, and that your fruit should remain, that whatever you ask the Father in My name He may give you." John 15:16

April 11

It's popular to be Christian and to be heathen, too.

> *"Depart, depart, go out from there, Touch nothing unclean; Go out of the midst of her, purify yourselves, You who carry the vessels of the Lord."* Isaiah 52:11 (NASB)

God says, "Your life cannot come in and out of the living word and be a life of insulation. It's the word that guards you and cleanses you."

> *Christ said, "You are already clean because of the word which I have spoken to you."* John 15:3

> *"...Christ also loved the church and gave Himself for her, that He might sanctify and cleanse her with the washing of water by the word, that He might present her to Himself a glorious church, not having spot or wrinkle or any such thing, but that she should be holy and without blemish."* Ephesians 5:25b-27

April 12

As believers and lovers of Christ, we are to express God wherever we go. We are to reflect His nature, His love, and His truth.

"O God, You are my God; early will I seek You; my soul thirsts for You; my flesh longs for You in a dry and thirsty land where there is no water. Because Your lovingkindness is better than life, my lips shall praise You. Thus will I bless You while I live; I will lift up my hands in Your name." Psalm 63:1,3-4

God says, "I want you to be who you are and who I want you to be in Christ—a living creature, a living personality, a living self that's a God self. My ultimate ambition is for you to be God selves."

"But you have not so learned Christ, if indeed you have heard Him and have been taught by Him, as the truth is in Jesus: that you put off, concerning your former conduct, the old man...And be renewed in the spirit of your mind, and that you put on the new man which was created according to God, in righteousness and true holiness." Ephesians 4:20-24

April 13

God says, "My Son is a standard, and you may not err from that standard. You must not even take a holy man's standard as your standard."

"For to this you were called, because Christ also suffered for us, leaving us an example, that you should follow His steps: Who committed no sin, nor was deceit found in His mouth."
1 Peter 2:21-22

God says, "Oh, let your ways be higher. Let your children even be in awe of what God is doing in you. Be gentle to one another, kindly affectioned. Harbor no bitterness or animosity toward yourselves or your children."

"But we were gentle among you, just as a nursing mother cherishes her own children. So, affectionately, longing for you, we were well pleased to impart to you not only the gospel of God, but also our own lives, because you had become dear to us." 1 Thessalonians 2:7-8

April 14

Christ says, "Your spirit must taste of Me personally, not of My words or My message, but of Me, of My essence, of My personality, of who I am. I am that I am. I'm the same yesterday, today, and forever. I'm standing before you, and you do not recognize your King is here."

"That I may know Him and the power of His resurrection, and the fellowship of His sufferings, being conformed to His death." Philippians 3:10

God says, "My heart has bled with mourning for those whose heads have been turned aside in the church world by their own importance."

"Therefore let him who thinks he stands take heed lest he fall." 1 Corinthians 10:12

April 15

God says, "I know your infirmities, and I'm moved by the feeling of your infirmities; and I intercede night and day through My Son for My beloved. Know that I am with you, and I will never leave you or forsake you!"

"Who is he who condemns? It is Christ who died, and furthermore is also risen, who is even at the right hand of God, who also makes intercession for us." Romans 8:34

God says, "My Christ has many things to give you, His promises that no one can give you but Him. He alone can give you eternal life. He alone can give you everything that pertains unto your salvation. He alone can confer upon you His love in a way that no man nor woman can love you in the world. Why settle for less than that which is the greatest and the highest thing in your life?"

"[That you may really come] to know [practically, through experience for yourselves] the love of Christ, which far surpasses mere knowledge [without experience]; that you may be filled [through all your being] unto all the fullness of God..." Ephesians 3:19 (AMP)

April 16

God says, "So there's a place in your daily regime of spiritual exercise to cast your care upon Me; and I cannot receive that care if you do not give it from your heart through your mouth. So you must have time daily to share with Me those things that are weighing upon you that you are feeling you have to shoulder alone."

"Casting the whole of your care [all your anxieties, all your worries, all your concerns, once and for all] on Him, for He cares for you affectionately and cares about you watchfully."
1 Peter 5:7 (AMP)

God says, "Cast upon Me that nature that's independent of God, which contributes to an antichrist predisposition for the enemy to come in and work through you."

"Cast away from you all the transgressions which you have committed, and get yourselves a new heart and a new spirit..." Ezekiel 18:31

"The work of righteousness will be peace, and the effect of righteousness, quietness and assurance forever." Isaiah 32:17

April 17

God says, "I love you with an everlasting love; and I secure for you freedom of the spirit to soar in the heavenlies. Freedom to choose to be a bondslave to Jesus. Freedom to receive the responsibilities of your calling under Christ. Freedom from the enemy from entanglement into bondage, that you may take the standard of the word."

> *"He brought them out of darkness and the shadow of death, and broke their chains in pieces."* Psalm 107:14

God says, "Let repentance come to the body of Christ all over the earth. Begin right now. Chasten the proud and haughty and indifferent, those who have no feelings for Me or who do not know how to express Me because they have never spent time in My presence. Until God moves among you, you will move in vain and be like stagnant waters. I will not take My Spirit away; but you must make My Spirit alive and be willing to pay all costs to let Me move among you."

> *"Repent therefore and be converted, that your sins may be blotted out, so that times of refreshing may come from the presence of the Lord."* Acts 3:19

April 18

God says, "You can either be a part of all the negative can'ts, or you can be a part of all the cans. Many men resign themselves to mediocrity and to being intimidated by the hand of the enemy. They speak from their circumstance and their condition."

God says the higher way is to speak from His perspective.

> *"...even God, who gives life to the dead and calls those things which do not exist as though they did."* Romans 4:17b

God says, "You are not to live in your circumstances, but you are to live as if your circumstances are not there. You are to live without even recognizing them."

> *"And Peter answered Him and said, 'Lord, if it is You, command me to come to You on the water.' So He said, 'Come.' And when Peter had come down out of the boat, he walked on the water to go to Jesus."* Matthew 14:28-29

April 19

God says, "I realize the heaviness you will feel when you feel inadequate to be where I want you, but that heaviness cannot work a work of bondage in you. It must work a sorrowful, godly work of repentance, that you may renounce and forbid these things from dominating and becoming your gods. Yea, you have freedom from them, and the freedom is found in repentance."

"If we confess our sins, He is faithful and just to forgive us our sins and to cleanse us from all unrighteousness." 1 John 1:9

God says, "When you confess to Me, My children, have I not removed them from you? Why would you feel that they are still weights upon your life? The flesh is not a weight upon you when you have been given forgiveness. When I have cleansed you from all unrighteousness as My word says, are you not free, then, of flesh? You're not in bondage then. I quicken you to be repentant unto Me and live. Let not the stain of sin or the cloud of weight and bondage rob you of your position with Me where you have freedom, and stand above sin through the cleansing that My Son brings in the Holy Spirit."

April 20

God asks, "How much time this week have you spent with Me? How much time have you spent in the spirit realm, as compared with the time you spent in the world around the carnality of the flesh?"

> *"Now as he reasoned about righteousness, self-control, and the judgment to come, Felix was afraid and answered, 'Go away for now; when I have a convenient time I will call for you.'"*
>
> Acts 24:25

Are we waiting for a convenient time to seek God?

God says, "Oh, My people, how I cry out for you to be a different people today; for I am ready to lead you into a land of plenty, but you can't wait until the doors are locked to come into My kingdom upon this earth. You cannot wait till then. You must go in at that time when I tell you. It is time, My people, to change your ways. It's time to come to the Lord and glorify Me, for I am God, and you are man. I made you out of clay that you may become spirit and truth. Become that which I have called you to be, and I will glorify Myself in you."

April 21

God says, "Realize that man's time is your enemy, and that God's time is your friend. I have forever. You have forever in your spirit as believers. You need to discover that a minute spent with God is like an eternal drop in an ocean of life. One little drop of time with Me becomes an ocean of eternity."

"Reverent and worshipful fear of the Lord is a fountain of life, that one may avoid the snares of death." Proverbs 14:27 (AMP)

God says, "Be good stewards of the time and breath I give you while living on this earth."

"If then you have been raised with Christ...aim at and seek the [rich, eternal treasures] that are above, where Christ is, seated at the right hand of God. And set your minds and keep them set on what is above (the higher things), not on the things that are on the earth." Colossians 3:1-2 (AMP)

April 22

God says, "Seek the biggest lifestyle you can—God's presence, God's purpose, God's power, God's glory. Seek Me, and you shall live."

"The Lord will guide you continually, and satisfy your soul in drought, and strengthen your bones; you shall be like a watered garden, and like a spring of water, whose waters do not fail."
Isaiah 58:11

God says, "Find out your cause for being here. Find out the purpose I've made you for, and do My will, and stop spending your time in the toy chest of the world. Stop presuming upon Me."

"...work out... your own salvation with reverence and awe and trembling (self-distrust, with serious caution, tenderness of conscience, watchfulness against temptation, timidly shrinking from whatever might offend God and discredit the name of Christ)." Philippians 2:12b (AMP)

April 23

Who believes in your potential more than God? The one who thinks the best of you is Jesus Christ.

"How precious also are Your thoughts to me, O God! How great is the sum of them! If I should count them, they would be more in number than the sand; when I awake, I am still with You." Psalm 139:17-18

God asks, "Do you not know that I planned your whole life from end to beginning and beginning to end? I know exactly what step you should take each day, every hour of the day, and every moment."

"Your eyes saw my unformed substance, and in Your book all the days [of my life] were written before ever they took shape, when as yet there was none of them." Psalm 139:16 (AMP)

April 24

Purpose is why you are here, but have faith that there is a greater purpose for your life than the one you can see.

> *"And we know that all things work together for good to those who love God, to those who are called according to His purpose. For whom He foreknew, He also predestined to be conformed to the image of His Son, that He might be the firstborn among many brethren."* Romans 8:28-29

God says, "I call you this day to a holy purpose, not to what the world is seeking. The destiny of the world is hell, the grave, and death. The destiny of the people of God is the spirit realm with rewards unthinkable and unsearchable with the presence of God in them at all times."

> *"You will show me the path of life; in Your presence is fullness of joy; at Your right hand are pleasures forevermore."* Psalm 16:11

April 25

God says, "For now I call upon you today to be great in your heart, great in your spirit, and great in your purpose; for your purpose is in Me."

> *"Then this Daniel distinguished himself...because an excellent spirit was in him..."* Daniel 6:3

> *"But Daniel purposed in his heart that he would not defile himself..."* Daniel 1:8a

God says, "The importance of being Mine is the most important ambition and calling of any man who says he's a truth seeker, a truth inspirer who wants to walk in My ways and commune with Me face to face in the cool of the day in God's presence."

> *"Only let your conduct be worthy of the gospel of Christ, so that whether I come and see you or am absent, I may hear of your affairs, that you stand fast in one spirit, with one mind striving together for the faith of the gospel."* Philippians 1:27

> *"So the Lord spoke to Moses face to face, as a man speaks to his friend."* Exodus 33:11

April 26

God says, "As you're beginning to complete your life on this earth and complete your purpose for being here, I want you to be like a river which will erode away everything that's hindering it and keeping it from getting to its destination. I want you to know no obstacle."

"And he showed me a pure river of water of life, clear as crystal, proceeding from the throne of God and of the Lamb." Revelation 22:1

God says, "Do not be moved by anything that is not of God. All that distracts is a battle plan of the enemy; but the battle plan of your heavenly Father is praise, peace, love, and joy in His purpose for you."

"...be strong and of good courage; be not afraid, nor be dismayed, for the Lord your God is with you wherever you go." Joshua 1:9

April 27

God says, "Preparation is spiritual, not physical. Preparation is the armament of God. The only time you can be prepared is now, and now should have been done yesterday. So, be alert and mobile, and prepare your heart, mind, soul, and strength to receive the King of kings."

"Finally, my brethren, be strong in the Lord and in the power of His might. Therefore take up the whole armor of God, that you may be able to withstand in the evil day, and having done all, to stand." Ephesians 6:10,13

God asks,
"When I call, will you be ready?"
"When I speak, will you hear?"
"When I return, will you be there?"

"For the promise is to you and to your children, and to all who are afar off, as many as the Lord our God will call." Acts 2:39

"...Go, lie down; and it shall be, if He calls you, that you must say, 'Speak, Lord, for Your servant hears.'" 1 Samuel 3:9

April 28

God says, "Do not forget that I have called you. Be ready, for I have said, 'Be alert and be mobile.' Drop all things to serve your King, for I have no other way for you to go than to go My way, regardless of what abilities you have."

> *"Many plans are in a man's mind, but it is the Lord's purpose for him that will stand."*
> Proverbs 19:21 (AMP)

Christ says, "My people, the time is so short. The hour is late, and I come swiftly. It is closer than you think. Those who are expectantly, eagerly waiting My return shall find Me, and I will not be one moment late when I come. I will be protective of them, and I will love them."

> *"Therefore, if anyone cleanses himself from the latter, he will be a vessel for honor, sanctified, useful for the Master, prepared for every good work."* 2 Timothy 2:21

> *"Therefore let us not sleep, as others do, but let us watch and be sober."* 1 Thessalonians 5:6

April 29

God asks, "Can you find one good thing in your past that is better than what I have for your future?"

> *"Now the Lord blessed the latter days of Job more than his beginning..."* Job 42:12a

> *"He saved us, not on the basis of deeds which we have done in righteousness, but according to His mercy, by the washing of regeneration and renewing by the Holy Spirit."* Titus 3:5 (NASB)

Never be afraid to trust an unknown future to a known God.

> *"Trust in the Lord, and do good; dwell in the land, and feed on His faithfulness. Delight yourself also in the Lord, and He shall give you the desires of your heart. Commit your way to the Lord, trust also in Him, and He shall bring it to pass."* Psalm 37:3-5

April 30

God says, "Children of promise, I speak to you as the Lord and Shepherd of your life. You have not been this way before. You won't be this way again. This is the only opportunity to serve Me in the now. You don't have the future. You don't have the past. You only have the present."

"But exhort one another daily, while it is called 'today,' lest any of you be hardened through the deceitfulness of sin. For we have become partakers of Christ if we hold the beginning of our confidence steadfast to the end."
Hebrews 3:13-14

God says, "I am the God that is of newness. Everything I do is a new thing in you."

"Therefore, we were buried with Him through baptism into death, that just as Christ was raised from the dead by the glory of the Father, even so we also should walk in newness of life."
Romans 6:4-5

May 1

God says, "My word is love. My principles are love, and they're meant to protect in an evil world."

"Because you have made the Lord, who is my refuge, even the Most High, your dwelling place, no evil shall befall you, nor shall any plague come near your dwelling; for He shall give His angels charge over you, to keep you in all your ways." Psalm 91:9-11

God says, "I never lead you to a place where I can't protect you. I love you, and I await your obedience."

"[Live] as children of obedience to God; do not conform yourselves to the evil desires [that governed you] in your former ignorance [when you did not know the requirements of the Gospel.]" 1 Peter 1:14 (AMP)

May 2

God says, "I will direct your paths. My paths are righteously safe and angelically guarded."

> "The steps of a good man are ordered by the Lord, and He delights in his way. Though he fall, he shall not be utterly cast down; for the Lord upholds him with His hand." Psalm 37:23-24

God can save us so much trouble.

> "So be subject to God. Resist the devil [stand firm against him], and he will flee from you. Come close to God and He will come close to you..." James 4:7-8a (AMP)

May 3

God says, "I've established My love before even you were born, before the foundation of the world. I knew you by name. You have no more safety than when you have a close relationship with Me."

> *"Because he has set his love upon Me, therefore*
> *I will deliver him; I will set him on high,*
> *because he has known My name."* Psalm 91:14

God says, "Who is the one who sees you have difficulty and warns you of things to come so you can be spared, and so, by intercession, you can be kept from the awful thing you are about to do?"

> *"Call to Me and I will answer you and show*
> *you great and mighty things, fenced in and*
> *hidden, which you do not know..."*
> Jeremiah 33:3 (AMP)

May 4

God asks, "Who in the universe would you rather please than your loving God, your Father who will be with you forever? And you will adore Me and worship Me, and I will hold you in My care forever, and nothing shall harm you."

"He who dwells in the secret place of the Most High shall abide under the shadow of the Almighty. I will say of the Lord, 'He is my refuge and my fortress; my God, in Him will I trust.'" Psalm 91:1-2

God says, "Let the door of your heart open. Only you can open the door. I stand there, and I knock. Sometimes you do not hear Me. Let Me in. You can't afford not to have Me with you at all times, because I'm better than any armament you can carry."

God asks, "What will you let go of tonight in order to gain Christ? What will you be willing to give up? Take Me."

May 5

God allows His people to be tested. He offers a promised land, then places a flooded river across its path and declares to His people: "Follow Me." God says tests and trials are necessary in our lives.

"Then the priests who bore the ark of the covenant of the Lord stood firm on dry ground in the midst of the Jordan; and all Israel crossed over on dry ground..." Joshua 3:17

God says, "You call them cares, tests, and troubles among each other. God calls them His opportunity to release His Spirit in that trouble."

We need to be in the grip of an indomitable spirit that overcomes all physical and mental handicaps and goes on.

When the enemy thinks we are at a standstill is the time we are to take a progressive step into God's very lifestyle.

God says, "Every day is important for you, for I have planned a victory for you."

May 6

God says, "As you are yoked to Me, I'm willing and able to shoulder all the burdens and pull all the load, but that's not My method, or you would not have spiritual maturity. My method is to allow you to be tested by letting your strength be used."

"Before I was afflicted I went astray, but now Your word do I keep [hearing, receiving, loving, and obeying it]." Psalm 119:67 (AMP)

"And Moses said to the people, 'Do not fear; for God has come to test you, and that His fear may be before you, so that you may not sin.'" Exodus 20:20

God says, "The storm clouds are gathering. The world is darkening, but the people of God are lightening, and their countenance is bright and full when they know who their God is, and they worship Me in spirit and truth. Begin to worship Me, and learn how to worship Me individually, as well as corporately. You do your part, and I'll do My part. My angels will then begin to carry on a praise and a *Shekinah* glory that cannot be heard. Do not stop, My people, but praise Me today."

May 7

God says, "If you will have the revelation understanding that I am with you in that situation, and if you will say, 'Christ Jesus, You are with me in this situation, therefore we cannot lose because You are the power of the Godhead.' Then say, 'I speak it in Your name, for without You I can do nothing.'"

"For it is God who works in you both to will and to do for His good pleasure." Philippians 2:13

"And you are complete in Him, who is the head of all principality and power." Colossians 2:10

God says, "I am your lifeline. I am your hope in present time of trouble. I am there in the time of crisis. I am there in the good times and the bad. I am there when the enemy is attacking you. I am waiting for you to call upon My strength, for My strength replaces your weakness."

"Be strong and of good courage, do not fear nor be afraid of them; for the Lord your God, He is the One who goes with you. He will not leave you nor forsake you." Deuteronomy 31:6

May 8

God says, "You can create the storms of your own making, because when you resign yourself to living under the threatening clouds, the testing clouds, the stormy trials, and you resign yourself to that, then you have given your permission for the enemy to obscure the light of the Son of God."

> *"Not only that, but we also glory in tribulations, knowing that tribulation produces perseverance; and perseverance, character; and character, hope. Now hope does not disappoint, because the love of God has been poured out in our hearts by the Holy Spirit who was given to us."* Romans 5:3-5

God says, "You can allow the storms of life and the tests and trials to obscure your sights of the spiritual. Then you cannot see beyond the circumstances so that you can only see as far as Satan lets you see, or you can decide you will not be a party to defeat from the enemy's hands."

> *"Therefore, My beloved brethren, be steadfast, immovable, always abounding in the work of the Lord, knowing that your labor is not in vain in the Lord."* 1 Corinthians 15:58

May 9

God says, "It takes spiritual vision and lofti-ness of where you are in the Spirit to enable you to see above the dark storm clouds in life. Can you see the Son of God?"

"But he, being full of the Holy Spirit, gazed into heaven and saw the glory of God, and Jesus standing at the right hand of God." Acts 7:55

"...but now we do not yet see all things put under Him. But we see Jesus..." Hebrews 2:8b-9a

In tests and trials, God wants us to become bet-ter, but the enemy wants us to become bitter.

"Pursue peace with all people, and holiness, without which no one will see the Lord: looking carefully lest anyone fall short of the grace of God; lest any root of bitterness springing up cause trouble, and by this many become defiled." Hebrews 12:14-15

May 10

Why do we think our life as a Christian will be without trial, discomfort, and endurance? God says all who live godly lives in Christ Jesus will suffer persecution. (See 2 Timothy 3:12.) But God is faithful to bring His people comfort and peace and joy in the midst of trial.

> *"And you shall be secure and feel confident because there is hope; yes, you shall search about you, and you shall take your rest in safety. You shall lie down, and none shall make you afraid..."* Job 11:18-19a (AMP)

God says, "Be aware I am testing the hearts of many. You think you've come far. You've just begun your journey."

> *"And you shall remember that the Lord your God led you all the way these forty years in the wilderness, to humble you and test you, to know what was in your heart, whether you would keep His commandments or not."* Deuteronomy 8:2

May 11

God speaks of suffering.

God says, "Perhaps you do not understand it completely. That is alright. I do not require that you understand anything completely. Let Me understand it for you."

"Now no chastening seems to be joyful for the present, but painful; nevertheless, afterward it yields the peaceable fruit of righteousness to those who have been trained by it." Hebrews 12:11

God says, "Trust the One Who never willed you to suffer or be hurt. Trust Me because I will deliver you, saith the Lord."

"And those who know Your name will put their trust in You; for You, Lord, have not forsaken those who seek You." Psalm 9:10

May 12

God says, "The soul that finds its rest in Me is the soul that will be all I intend your character to be. I alone can give you rest. Now be at rest and be about your Father's business."

> *"There remains therefore a rest for the people of God. For he who has entered His rest has himself also ceased from his works as God did from His. Let us therefore be diligent to enter that rest..."* Hebrews 4:9-11a

The Lord is the strength of my life, and I must enter His rest by choosing to be about my Father's business.

> *"For You have been a shelter for me, and a strong tower from the enemy. I will abide in Your tabernacle forever, I will trust in the shelter of Your wings. Selah."* Psalm 61:3-4

God has painted a beautiful picture of rest for His people.

May 13

God says, "Being at peace with yourself is a direct result of finding peace with God. When you have nothing to hide, you have peace inside."

*"And let the peace (soul harmony which comes)
from Christ rule (act as an umpire continually)
in your hearts [deciding and settling with
finality all questions that arise in your minds..."*
Colossians 3:15 (AMP)

God says, "Until you're at peace with yourself, do not seek peace with others, because it becomes an issue with your relationships. When peace is solidly controlling your heart, then My joy and My liberty shall be yours."

*"...He who would love life and see good days,
...Let him turn away from evil and do good;
Let him seek peace and pursue it."* 1 Peter 3:10-11

May 14

God says, "Be aware that I have not been the author of your confusion, but rather I have been the author of your peace. Except you embrace the peace that I give you, you must seek your peace in Me."

"For God is not the author of confusion but of peace..." 1 Corinthians 14:33

"...in Me you may have peace. In the world you will have tribulation; but be of good cheer, I have overcome the world." John 16:33

The peace of Christ which passes all understanding is all you need, because His peace is greater than understanding.

"Be anxious for nothing, but in everything by prayer and supplication, with thanksgiving, let your requests be made known to God; and the peace of God, which surpasses all understanding, will guard your hearts and minds through Christ Jesus." Philippians 4:6-7

May 15

God says, "That peace which passes all understanding is the continual presence of My living word in you, prospering and growing and doing well and forming the Son, the living bread, in you and conforming you to that image."

"For we are His workmanship, created in Christ Jesus for good works, which God prepared beforehand that we should walk in them." Ephesians 2:9-10

God says, "You are to seek that peace that passes all understanding, that passes all comprehension, that passes the need to be concerned with what goes on around you. I've yearned for you to sit content with Me. I've yearned for you to be satisfied with your fellowship and My fellowship as one. I've set the garden of your heart to be reserved for Me and Me alone."

"You will keep him in perfect peace, whose mind is stayed on You, because he trusts in You." Isaiah 26:3

May 16

God says, "Keep your peace. Keep your peace. At all costs, keep your peace. Be a peacemaker at all costs."

God does not mean we are to keep peace by expediency or compromise. He means we are to speak and act at the right time in the right spirit.

> *"How beautiful upon the mountains are the feet*
> *of him who brings good news, who proclaims*
> *peace, who brings glad tidings of good things..."*
> Isaiah 52:7

God says, "Have done with that lesser principle focus you have on the day-by-day situations which will always point you to a problem, always remind you there's tension, always try to get you to anticipate an evil thing like stress, fear, concern, worry, or pain."

God wants to see our own lives fading into the background.

> *"...Let him search for peace (harmony; undis-*
> *turbedness from fears, agitating passions and*
> *moral conflicts) and seek it eagerly..."*
> 1 Peter 3:11b (AMP)

May 17

God says, "Every word that has been spoken of in My *logos*, I spoke, and I have faithful men who have recorded those words, and I have not finished speaking. I still speak today. I want My sons to live by every word that proceeds out of My mouth. Have I not called My beloved Son, Jesus, the Word?"

"And truly Jesus did many other signs in the presence of His disciples, which are not written in this book." John 20:30

God says, "You must know that there is no other way that you will grow in this last day than to feed on the *logos* (written word) and the *rhema* (spoken word); because it is that two-edged sword which will cause the work to be done against the enemy. The enemy fears mightily those who walk in *logos* and *rhema*, and those who are trained in that."

"The entirety of Your word is truth, and every one of Your righteous judgments endures forever. Great peace have those who love Your law, and nothing causes them to stumble."
Psalm 119:160,165

May 18

God says, "The entire word, both written and yet to be spoken, is contained in the person of My Son."

God says to look upon His Son, "the centrality of Jesus, who is the life-giver, the word-giver, the truth-giver."

> *" 'I am the Alpha and the Omega, the*
> *Beginning and the End,' says the Lord, 'who is*
> *and who was and who is to come, the*
> *Almighty.'"* Revelation 1:8

God says, "You received My word of salvation, now receive My word of life and let your spirit grow. Let your faith grow through My word, and practice My word daily. Don't just confess it, My children. Live by it. Put it into action. Believe it. Convince yourself that it is truth, and the only true thing you have."

> *"For the law was given through Moses, but*
> *grace and truth came through Jesus Christ."*
> John 1:17

May 19

God says, "To begin to divide the spirit and soul, you must have the two-edged sword. It must not be the *logos*, but the *rhema* and *logos* combined and immersed together as one word. All of My word is *rhema*, because even that which you say is *logos*, once it is within your mouth and in your spirit and heart, it is *rhema*."

"He had in His right hand seven stars, out of His mouth went a two-edged sword, and His countenance was like the sun shining in its strength." Revelation 1:16

God says, "You are rising, but you have not invaded the spiritual realm in the sense that you have fully divested your spirit from any control by the flesh, or the soul, or the mind—the will, emotions and intellect. And so, the only way this can be done is living in the reality of My *rhema* and My *logos* dwelling fully in such a manner that it shall become the only reality you know."

"But the word is very near you, in your mouth and in your heart, that you may do it."
Deuteronomy 30:14

May 20

God says, "The world of the word includes that which is written and that which is spoken and revealed; and they together form a twin communion for the spirit and soul of man."

"For the Word that God speaks is alive and full of power [making it active, operative, energizing, and effective]; it is sharper than any two-edged sword, penetrating to the dividing line of the breath of life (soul) and [the immortal] spirit, and of joints and marrow [of the deepest parts of our nature], exposing and sifting and analyzing and judging the very thoughts and purposes of the heart." Hebrews 4:12 (AMP)

God says, "Listen to My words, and listen carefully, because only by tasting and learning and meditating and assimilating all these things in your heart will you be able to put on the full armor of not *logos*, but *rhema* which will cover you completely and seal you as it did the Hebrew children in the fire."

May 21

God says, "It is the spirit that should feed the soul. It should never be your physical eyes that feed the soul. It should be the Spirit of truth."

God's order is for the spirit to rule the soul and body. The soul that is not ruled is a bully. God says the soul needs salvation also.

> *"Therefore lay aside all filthiness and overflow of wickedness, and receive with meekness the implanted word, which is able to save your souls."* James 1:21

God says, "Do not look at things as they appear to be until you have been thoroughly purged from receiving what pleases the soul, until you begin to seek to see spiritually what pleases the Spirit. Those things which please the Spirit are not of this world."

> *"And if your eye causes you to sin, pluck it out and cast it from you. It is better for you to enter into life with one eye, rather than having two eyes, to be cast into hell fire."* Matthew 18:9

> *"My eyes are ever toward the Lord..."* Psalm 25:15

May 22

God says, "Your soul is very biased and receives only the things it wants to receive. It is not a reliable barometer of what is taking place around you."

"For all that is in the world—the lust of the flesh, the lust of the eyes, and the pride of life—is not of the Father but is of the world."
1 John 2:16

God says, "The eye is roaming to and fro seeking that which is pleasurable to the soul, and so, the eye is literally in bondage to the soul."

"Hell and Destruction are never full; So the eyes of man are never satisfied." Proverbs 27:20

God says to train the spiritual eye which will focus only on those things that will edify the inner man of the spirit.

May 23

God says, "I ordain that you come into a new level of response and stop saying in your soulish area that I am having this or that or the other which is preventing me from doing this or that or the other."

"I have strength for all things in Christ Who empowers me [I am ready for anything and equal to anything through Him Who infuses inner strength into me; I am self-sufficient in Christ's sufficiency]." Philippians 4:13 (AMP)

God says, "The soul must be perfected by the engrafted word. The engrafted word is one which will settle things in your hearts, so that there will be no division between soul and mind and heart, but there will be a unity between the soul-heart complex, not between the soul-mind complex, because your minds are not yet renewed."

"For You will light my lamp; the Lord my God will enlighten my darkness." Psalm 18:28

May 24

God designed His children to be tripartite beings—spirit, soul, and body. We are spirits who have a soul and live in a body.

God's spiritual principle of order is: spirit responding to the word, soul agreeing with the word, and the body following.

"And you shall love the Lord your God with all your [mind and] heart and with your entire being and with all your might."
Deuteronomy 6:5 (AMP)

God says, "I must be allowed to draw the mind into the direction of the spirit, and the body in the direction of the spirit by My word and Spirit."

"By this we know that we abide in Him, and He in us, because He has given us of His Spirit." 1 John 4:13

"The Spirit of truth whom the world cannot receive, because it neither sees Him, nor knows Him, but you know Him, for He dwells with you and will be in you." John 14:17

He is Jesus Christ, the Living Word!

May 25

God says, "I desire that your whole body, mind, and spirit be blameless and perfected. I desire that you win victory over the flesh—your body, your mind, your emotions. I desire that they conform to the revealed word. They will not conform to your word. If your word is all that is in you, be assured that My perfection will not be in your flesh; but if My revealed word is in you, and you have submitted to it totally, then you will see changes in the flesh."

"The Lord knows the thoughts of man, that they are futile." Psalm 94:11

God says, "Bring your body and mind into conformity to the word, and the spirit will agree and change the body and mind into a perfected state. Then you'll have the hundredfold blessing."

"But he who received seed on the good ground is he who hears the word and understands it, who indeed bears fruit and produces: some a hundredfold, some sixty, some thirty." Matthew 13:23

"...I will put My laws into their hearts, and in their minds I will write them." Hebrews 10:16b

May 26

God says, "The heart of man is a dilemma to those who don't understand the heart nature. People always think of the heart as some unknown quantity when it is a quality of spirit. The heart is the link between spirit and mind, and you have to have that channel cleansed."

"Keep and guard your heart with all vigilance and above all that you guard, for out of it flow the springs of life." Proverbs 4:23 (AMP)

God says, "So these things in your mind–soul–heart complex must be cast upon Me when you're helpless and not able to rise above your situation, for I understand."

God says to give Him that nature that is independent of God.

"And the Lord said to Moses, 'I have seen this people, and indeed it is a stiffnecked people!'"
Exodus 32:9

May 27

God says, "Your spirit is willing. It is your flesh that is weak; but remember that the flesh is weak, so you can overcome it."

"But the end of all things is at hand; therefore be serious and watchful in your prayers." 1 Peter 4:7

"And they overcame him by the blood of the Lamb and by the word of their testimony, and they did not love their lives to the death."
Revelation 12:11

Believers are to will their lives to be crucified.

God says, "In order to please Me, you cannot please your soul. In order to please the evil one, you must please the soul. So begin to imagine spiritual things within the reality of your soul."

"Finally, brethren, whatever things are true, whatever things are noble, whatever things are just, whatever things are pure, whatever things are lovely, whatever things are of good report, if there is any virtue and if there is anything praiseworthy—meditate on those things."
Philippians 4:8

May 28

God says, "The hedge of the spirit is always up, but maybe the hedge around the body is down. You see, there can be that possibility. The hedge of the mind can be down and the hedge of the spirit up. And so there are unequal things going on, tripartitely speaking."

"Though one may be overpowered by another, two can withstand him. And a threefold cord is not quickly broken." Ecclesiastes 4:12

Spirit responds—mind agrees—body follows!

God says, "What I will take, as a willing sacrifice unto Me holy and acceptable, is a willing spirit. That means to give Me a spirit of harmony with the word, and allow the body to be an outcome of My word, and your mind to be an outcome of the spirit's direction."

"And be renewed in the spirit of your mind."
Ephesians 4:23

"How shall a young man cleanse his way? By taking heed and keeping watch [on himself] according to Your word [conforming his life to it]." Psalm 119:9 (AMP)

May 29

God says, "Why recrucify you the Christ, the Son of God?"

We recrucify Christ when we reject Him and reject what He has done for us, when we don't accept His unconditional love and forgiveness for us. We wound Him again when we turn from His way.

> *"For it is impossible for those who were once enlightened, and have tasted the heavenly gift, and have become partakers of the Holy Spirit...if they fall away, to renew them again to repentance, since they crucify again for themselves the Son of God, and put Him to an open shame."* Hebrews 6:4,6

God asks, "Will you bend your pride to Me? Will you bend your stubbornness to Me, your resistance to Me, your apathy to Me—or will you stand in your flesh and refuse to accept the calling I have on your life?"

> *"...fear not, for I have redeemed you; I have called you by your name; you are Mine."*
> Isaiah 43:1b

May 30

God says, "Anyone that comes to Me must come to Me under My terms."

We cannot set up our own agenda for we deceive ourselves.

> *"Woe to the rebellious children, says the Lord,*
> *who take counsel but not of Me, and who*
> *devise plans, but not of My Spirit, that they*
> *may add sin to sin."* Isaiah 30:1

God says, "You cannot organize Me, but I can disorganize you, and then I can organize you according to My will. You must be clay in the potter's hand, but every time I feel resistance by My Spirit in your being, I am not willing to take the kingdom of yourself by storm."

> *"And the vessel that he made of clay was*
> *marred in the hand of the potter; so he made it*
> *again into another vessel, as it seemed good to*
> *the potter to make... 'O house of Israel, can I*
> *not do with you as this potter?' says the Lord.*
> *'Look, as the clay is in the potter's hand, so are*
> *you in My hand...'"* Jeremiah 18:4,6

May 31

The only truly safe place to be is inside the will of God. Our safe place is not where we live, but it is in Whom we live. God says we have no more safety than when we have a close relationship with Him.

> *"That you may love the Lord your God, that you may obey His voice, and that you may cling to Him, for He is your life and the length of your days..."* Deuteronomy 30:20a

Are you obeying every word that comes from the mouth of God (Matthew 4:4), or are you saying, "That's wonderful, and I know that's God, but as for me and my house, I can't?"

God says, "You want to hear from God, but then when you hear from God, what do you do with what I say?"

> *"...It is written, 'Man shall not live by bread alone, but by every word of God.'"* Luke 4:4

June 1

Habits are so slowly lost because you have lifelong customs that you think give you a choice of freedom from the will of God.

"For when you were slaves of sin, you were free in regard to righteousness. But then what benefit (return) did you get from the things of which you are now ashamed? [None] for the end of those things is death." Romans 6:20-21 (AMP)

What is sin to you?

1. Sin obscures your awareness of God.
2. Sin impairs the tenderness of your conscience.
3. Sin weakens your ability to reason as God says.
4. Sin increases the authority of your mind over your body.
5. Sin restrains your hunger for spiritual truth.

No matter how innocent sin may seem, it is still sin, for whatever is not of faith is sin. (See Romans 14:23.)

June 2

God says, "Your spirit man suffers when you sin. You mar his beautiful brightness that's there for sinlessness. The more you sin, the more you offend your spirit."

"For thus says the High and Lofty One who inhabits eternity, whose name is Holy: 'I dwell in the high and holy place, with him who has a contrite and humble spirit, to revive the spirit of the humble, and to revive the heart of the contrite ones.'" Isaiah 57:15

God says, "In our liberal economy, people believe it's alright, it's alright, it's alright, it's alright, it's alright. Right by men's standards is wrong. Only right by God's standard is right."

"For the time will come when they will not endure sound doctrine, but according to their own desires, because they have itching ears, they will heap up for themselves teachers."
2 Timothy 4:3-4

June 3

God says, "Yes, the enemy is the author of sin and sickness and calamity, but it's not that I allow him. My people allow him by not getting rid of sin in the temples that should be Mine."

> *"Or do you not know that your body is the temple of the Holy Spirit who is in you, whom you have from God, and you are not your own? For you were bought at a price; therefore glorify God in your body and in your spirit, which are God's."* 1 Corinthians 6:19-20

If you don't hate evil, you'll be more lukewarm than hot and more likely to sin than not. The Scripture tells us that if we love the Lord, we are to hate evil. (See Proverbs 8:13.) It takes hatred of evil to resist all that the world puts before us.

> *(David cried out in the Psalms) "Do I not hate them, O Lord, who hate You? And do I not loathe those who rise up against You? I hate them with perfect hatred; I count them my enemies."* Psalm 139:21-22

June 4

God says, "The sin that is not forgivable is the sin that is not given to Me, confessed to Me or identified to Me."

If one chooses not to identify or confess the sin to God, the sin still remains.

> *"Confess your trespasses to one another, and pray for one another, that you may be healed. The effective, fervent prayer of a righteous man avails much."* James 5:16

God says, "True repentance is a change of all the nature tripartitely—spirit, soul, and body. It is a complete 180-degree change. True repentance says, 'I have done all I need or can do.'"

Tell God you want a godly sorrow produced in your life. Decide you want to choose to mourn over sin.

> *"So David said, 'While the child was still alive, I fasted and wept; for I said, "Who can tell whether the Lord will be gracious to me, that the child may live?" But now he is dead; why should I fast? Can I bring him back again? I shall go to him; but he shall not return to me.'"*
> 2 Samuel 12:22-23

June 5

God says, "Desire to have your heart broken over sin. Ask for this and realize you have compromised the word, quenched and grieved the heart of God."

We need full repentance—to agonize with tears, travailing and grieving over our sin.

> *"Draw near to God and He will draw near to you. Cleanse your hands, you sinners; and purify your hearts...lament and mourn and weep!...humble yourselves in the sight of the Lord, and He will lift you up."* James 4:8-10

God says, "Put away the sin, and the obstacle will go, and the light will come, and it will be purifying, and the light will produce a high standard of holiness, and the light will also produce the presence of My Son. Light cannot come in and dispel darkness until sin is put away. Sin is the obstacle."

Our part is to put away the sin.

> *"...God is light and in Him is no darkness at all."* 1 John 1:5b

June 6

We will continue to sin unless we take steps to see as God sees and to see God as He is.

1. We must see sin as God sees it, with spiritual eyes. We must have an increased hatred of evil.
2. We must see how much we vex, quench, grieve and resist the Godhead. Remember, our sin is against God only.
3. We need a greater revelation of God's love, mercy, tenderness, and forgiveness, even while we sin.

"Would not God search this out? For He knows the secrets of the heart." Psalm 44:21

God says, "Darkness is darkness, and light is light. God is God, and sin is sin. Do you not know the difference?"

God asks, "Do you think My Spirit would hesitate to show you sin and where repentance must be?"

"...the Holy Spirit will convict the world of sin, and of righteousness, and of judgment." John 16:8

"As many as I love, I rebuke and chasten. Therefore be zealous and repent." Revelation 3:19

June 7

God says, "Rebellion is as the sin of witchcraft. It's the act of sorcery, because you've been deluded. You've been deceived. Your eyes are blind. You cannot hear, and you will not believe the truth and come to Me, that you may be healed."

"For rebellion is as the sin of witchcraft, and stubbornness is as iniquity and idolatry. Because you have rejected the word of the Lord, He also has rejected you from being king." 1 Samuel 15:23

"There are those who rebel against the light; they do not know its ways nor abide in its paths." Job 24:13

God says, "Flee evil but not in fear. Flee in a fear of God that says, I cannot bear to hurt God or quench His Spirit."

"Then they will call on Me, but I will not answer; they will seek Me diligently, but they will not find Me. Because they hated knowledge and did not choose the fear of the Lord, they would have none of My counsel and despised all My reproof. But whoever listens to Me will dwell safely, and will be secure, without fear of evil." Proverbs 1:28-30, 33

June 8

Christ says, "I have become your sinbearer so you need not think of your sin today. It's in the past, and it's under the blood. And you need not remind each other of your pasts."

"And from Jesus Christ the faithful and trust-worthy Witness...To Him Who ever loves us and has once [for all] loosed and freed us from our sins by His own blood." Revelation 1:5 (AMP)

God says, "You can stand upright today as if you've never sinned."

" 'Come now, and let us reason together,' says the Lord, 'Though your sins are like scarlet, they shall be as white as snow; though they are red like crimson, they shall be as wool.'" Isaiah 1:18

June 9

God asks, "Are you able to identify the imperfection? If perfection is not working in that area, are you to say that I, your Father, have somehow overlooked or decided by My perfect will I would not perfect you there? Rather, you must decide that it is your Father's good pleasure to give you the kingdom."

"...let us lay aside every weight, and the sin which so easily ensnares us, and let us run with endurance the race that is set before us, looking unto Jesus, the author and finisher of our faith..." Hebrews 12:1b-2a

Christ Jesus is the perfecting Word.

God asks, "Are you tired of this life in the flesh? Your Father is wanting you to have a bad taste for things of the world. He's wanting you to grow up and see that all that froth and all that clay is nothing but the lust of the flesh, lust of the eyes, and pride of life. Seek not to embellish yourself with enjoyment in the flesh, for that takes you from the Spirit."

"Whoever finds his [lower] life will lose it [the higher life], and whoever loses his [lower] life on My account will find it [the higher life]."
Matthew 10:39 (AMP)

June 10

God asks, "Why is it sin? Because to know what is right to do and to do it not is detracting from My word, because it's a passive rejection of My word by the sins of omission."

"If we say that we have not sinned, we make Him a liar, and His word is not in us."
1 John 1:10

"But everyone who hears these sayings of Mine, and does not do them, will be like a foolish man who built his house on the sand." Matthew 7:26

God says, "Sin will wink at sin. Sin will ignore sin. Sin will say, 'One day it will be better.'"

"Then Saul said, 'I have sinned; yet honor me now, please, before the elders of my people and before Israel, and return with me...'"
1 Samuel 15:30

"Oh, that you had heeded My commandments! Then your peace would have been like a river, and your righteousness like the waves of the sea." Isaiah 48:18

June 11

God says, "Do not be surprised at those things about you which cause you to be caught up in the tumult of everyday living. Do not be surprised at how the manipulator of this society you live in manipulates people around you to try to change the course of events in your lives. Only be glad that I have brought you apart."

"A man who has friends must himself be friendly, but there is a friend who sticks closer than a brother." Proverbs 18:24

God says, "For those you once thought were your close friends and standing with you, some of those friends will suddenly turn the other way. That happens all the time, but those true friends will not turn from you. They will stand with you, and they will love you, and they will believe in what I have caused you to do. With a sincere heart of love, they would serve the King of kings. You will know them by their fruits. If they are truly your friends, they will not hinder My Spirit in you. They will not bring confusion in you. They will not bring unrest in you. Rather, they will bring peace, joy, longsuffering, patience, meekness, and temperance."

June 12

God says, "Don't you realize that I have not called you to be in the majority? I have called you to walk like I walked on this earth: to walk sometimes misunderstood and alone. Sometimes you will have to go off to the mountain and pray all night. Sometimes even your own closest friends will not understand, but do you know that they will come when you will stand with Me? I will say, 'Well done, thou good and faithful servant,' because you will have many rewards in My kingdom because you have put Me first."

"Greater love has no one than this, than to lay down one's life for his friends. You are My friends if you do whatever I command you."
John 15:13-14

God says, "You will be shown people that will come to support and stand with you, and these people will be genuine, true friends of Christ. They will not be hypocritical. They will not have any motive in mind. They will want to love you and be your friend because they are of God; and things of God gravitate to each other."

June 13

God says, "When you choose to let the flesh have its own way, you pay a huge price. It's the law of sowing and multiplied reaping."

There are many temptations and desires in life to please your *self*. The temptation is that you won't love God more than you love your sin.

"For all seek their own, not the things which are of Christ Jesus." Philippians 2:21

"But clothe yourself with the Lord Jesus Christ (the Messiah) and make no provisions for [indulging] the flesh..." Romans 13:14 (AMP)

God says, "You are not able in your flesh to escape temptation but you are able in your spirit. A Christian life is one of enduring temptations."

"Blessed is the man who endures temptation; for when he has been approved, he will receive the crown of life which the Lord has promised to those who love Him." James 1:12

June 14

God says, "Growth is the only way a Christian can avoid temptation—by growing in the area of saying no."

God says, "The temptation is not the problem. The problem is your will against Satan's will. You must say, 'Get thee behind me, Satan.'"

> *"But Jesus turned and said to Peter, 'Get behind Me, Satan! You are an offense to Me, for you are not mindful of the things of God, but of the things of men.'"* Matthew 16:23

God says, "Temptation leads to sin when you act upon it. Temptation leads to spiritual growth when you refuse it."

Entering into temptation is your will. Resisting temptation is God's will. God gives us the ability to obey Him.

> *"Now if [all these things be true, then be sure] the Lord knows how to rescue the godly out of temptations and trials..."* 2 Peter 2:9a (AMP)

June 15

God says we are to say, "When I am weak, I am strong, because the strength of my Lord is in me in that area."

God says, "The life you live in that area of My word you live by the faith of the Son of God, who loves you and gives Himself for you in His perfecting power that you may be perfected." (See Galatians 2:20.)

> *"It is God who arms me with strength, and*
> *makes my way perfect."* Psalm 18:32

God says, "I give you a way out of evil. I give you the ability to say no. When it comes down to it, you don't have to say yes to the enemy. You can say no."

The true test of a Christian is, "Can you resist the enemy?"

> *"You shall not consent to him or listen to him,*
> *nor shall your eye pity him, nor shall you spare*
> *him or concel him."* Deuteronomy 13:8

June 16

God says, "I have no worldliness to give you today, for if you would be a friend of the world, you are definitely My enemy, so whatever is of the world in you has become hostile to Me."

"...Do you not know that being the world's friend is being God's enemy? So whoever chooses to be a friend of the world takes his stand as an enemy of God." James 4:4b (AMP)

God says, "You are either in the word, and the word is conforming you to the image of Jesus Christ, or you are in the world, and the world is conforming you to its mold."

"And do not be conformed to this world, but be transformed by the renewing of your mind, that you may prove what is that good and acceptable and perfect will of God." Romans 12:2

June 17

God says, "To not succeed in the world is sometimes better for your inner man because when you succeed in the world, you sometimes leave Me alone; you sometimes ignore Me." God says that is when you need Him most.

"Now am I trying to win the favor of men, or of God? Do I seek to please men? If I were still seeking popularity with men, I should not be a bond servant of Christ..." Galatians 1:10 (AMP)

"Then Peter and the apostles replied, We must obey God rather than men." Acts 5:29 (AMP)

God says, "Whatever the society is recommending, that should be your clue to flee from it."

"But far be it from me to glory [in anything or anyone] except in the cross of our Lord Jesus Christ (the Messiah), through Whom the world has been crucified to me, and I to the world!"
Galatians 6:14 (AMP)

June 18

God says, "Do not have the inordinate love for the world that you should not have. Do not have the excessive addiction to the ways of the world because the world is your enemy."

"Do not love the world or the things in the world. If anyone loves the world, the love of the Father is not in him." 1 John 2:15

God says, "Your love must not be with the world anymore. It should have passed when you came into My kingdom."

"And the world is passing away, and the lust of it; but he who does the will of God abides forever." 1 John 2:17

June 19

God says, "The world cannot give you rest. The world cannot meet your need. The world will complicate your life. I will ease your life and make it simple, because the love of God is stronger than any love relationship you can have in this world. Be persuaded that all God has is love for you. All God has is peace for you. All God has is His nature for you."

"Therefore 'Come out from among them and be separate, says the Lord. Do not touch what is unclean, and I will receive you.'"
2 Corinthians 6:17

God says, "Say no to the nature of the world that has captivated you and caused you to think the world is more important to you than your God. The world is nothing, for if you gain the whole world and lose your own soul, what profit is there?" (See Matthew 16:26.)

God says, "So you cannot achieve anything in this world, but what I will call you to account for is what you've not achieved in Me."

June 20

God says, "You have a full right to enter in and embrace and relish the darkness and sin of the world. It's not My choice for you, but I give you the right to choose for yourself. My choice is for you to be the object of My love, completely clean and forgiven. I see you as a restored vessel, and I want you as My beloved."

A carnal Christian is one who has accepted the message of salvation, but his lifestyle and priorities are directed by preoccupation with himself. He looks more like the world of non-Christians than like Christ.

You must value what you believe, and value it so strongly that you internalize it and act upon it.

God says, "Others will look to you to see if you are changed by the power of God in your life. They will not look to the Book if you are not walking epistles."

June 21

God says, "Yielding to Me leads not only to dedication but also separation. (See Romans 12:2.) Since the world is resolutely opposed to Me, one cannot revel in its lusts and at the same time do My will." (See 1 John 2:15-17.)

Separation from the world involves being "unfashionable" in spirit, thoughts, values and actions according to the world's standards.

God calls you to fast from the cares of this world and from the physical and soulish environment. God says the purest form of fasting is where you are totally withdrawn from all influences and intrusions into your communication with Him.

God says, "Your body must be so subdued before your conquering spirit that it has no ability to intrude into your spirit communication with Me."

" 'Therefore also now,' says the Lord, 'turn and keep on coming to Me with all your heart, with fasting, with weeping, and with mourning [until every hindrance is removed and the broken fellowship is restored].'" Joel 2:12 (AMP)

June 22

God says, "There has to be a god of this world in order for there to be a choice between the God of your world and the god of this world. You see the God of your world is Me. The god of this world is Satan."

"I call heaven and earth as witnesses today against you, that I have set before you life and death, blessing and cursing; therefore choose life, that both you and your descendants may live."
Deuteronomy 30:19

God defines lust:

"Lust of the eyes: Oh, that looks good!

Lust of the flesh: I've got to have that!

Pride of life: I have a right to have that!

Be a whole and holy instrument to Me."

June 23

We are the caretakers of our own hearts, with the help of the Holy Spirit. God says there's an inner heart, and it cannot handle the beating it gets from the exposure to the carnal world.

God says, "You first need a heart after Me. Then I can clean it up and lead you to a quiet place of refuge, away from all that would distract."

> *"Then I will give them a heart to know Me, that I am the Lord; and they shall be My people, and I will be their God, for they shall return to Me with their whole heart."* Jeremiah 24:7

God says, "That which is corrupt is corruptive in its influence, but that which is perfect is perfect in its influence. Do not be satisfied with producing only a mixture of good and evil. Does a good fountain bring forth evil and good water at the same time? No, it cannot. Either make the fountain good or make the fountain evil. Well, the fountain of your mouth, and the fountain of your hands, the fountain of your mind and heart must be good, or it will produce corruptive fruit."

> *"Even so, every good tree bears good fruit, but a bad tree bears bad fruit."* Matthew 7:17

June 24

Christ has stringent rules to live by—He doesn't make it easy.

> *"Enter by the narrow gate; for wide is the gate, broad is the way that leads to destruction, and there are many who go in by it. Because narrow is the gate and difficult is the way which leads to life, and there are few who find it."*
> Matthew 7:13-14

It only takes a heart after God, and the things of the world lose their hold on us.

> *"Then Jesus spoke to them again, saying, 'I am the light of the world. He who follows Me shall not walk in darkness, but have the light of life.'"*
> John 8:12

God says, "You can walk and not stumble in that light. You will feel clean, because the light cleanses you."

> *"He has delivered us from the power of darkness and translated us into the kingdom of the Son of His love."* Colossians 1:13

June 25

God says, "Break forth as you sing in joy. Break forth in peace. Break forth in love, and let the world cease to have control over you, but be you rather controlled by Me, for I am the Father who never changes."

"For you shall go out with joy, and be led out with peace; the mountains and the hills shall break forth into singing before you, and all the trees of the field shall clap their hands."
Isaiah 55:12

God says, "My children, how I love you. How poor you are, and you realize that the end of yourself is in trusting in yourself, and how inadequate you feel at these times. I allow you to go through these things to show you, you will never make it without Me."

"But Jesus looked at them and said to them, 'With men this is impossible, but with God all things are possible.'" Matthew 19:26

June 26

God says, "Satan is not My adversary. I am not in a position to have an adversary. Satan is your adversary. His intention is to prosper you wickedly."

> *"Be sober, be vigilant; because your adversary the devil walks about like a roaring lion, seeking whom he may devour. Resist him, steadfast in the faith..."* 1 Peter 5:8-9a

God says, "Satan will strike wherever there is vulnerability. He loves to keep you in a quandary. He enjoys the quandary you're in."

The purpose of letting Satan have at you is to conquer him in you.

> *(The Lord said to Cain)* *" 'If you do well, will not your countenance be lifted up? And if you do not do well, sin is crouching at the door; and its desire is for you, but you must master it.' Cain told Abel his brother. And it came about when they were in the field, that Cain rose up against Abel and killed him."* Genesis 4:7-8 (NASB)

Cain did not heed God and attempt to conquer Satan and master the sin crouching at his door.

June 27

God says, "If Satan didn't have beauty about him, you wouldn't be attracted to him. As far back as Eve, he has made evil attractive."

"So when the woman saw that the tree was good for food, that it was pleasant to the eyes, and a tree desirable to make one wise, she took of its fruit and ate. She also gave to her husband with her and he ate." Genesis 3:6

"And no wonder! For Satan himself transforms himself into an angel of light."
2 Corinthians 11:14

God says, "The enemy will come in his disguises as an angel of light to tempt you, to try to lead you from the tree of life, and not to it."

"Now the serpent was more cunning than any beast of the field which the Lord God had made. And he said to the woman, 'Has God indeed said, you shall not eat of every tree of the garden?'" Genesis 3:1

"So God drove out the man; and He placed cherubim at the east of the garden of Eden, and a flaming sword which turned every way, to guard the way to the tree of life." Genesis 3:24

June 28

God says, "When you yield to temptation, you make a black mark on your soul that can't be removed except by sorrow and repentance. Satan, disguised as an angel of light, seeks to wear down your resistance to temptation."

"For godly sorrow produces repentance to salvation, not to be regretted...for observe this very thing, that you sorrowed in a godly manner: what diligence it produced in you, what clearing of yourselves...what vehement desire, what zeal..." 2 Corinthians 7:10-11

The devil has the audacity to tell you he is speaking for God. His job is to tempt believers to turn their backs on God.

Christ is always there when we are tempted.

"But I fear, lest somehow, as the serpent deceived Eve by his craftiness, so your minds may be corrupted from the simplicity that is in Christ." 2 Corinthians 11:3

June 29

God says, "If any flesh is seen in you, the enemy will be glad to invade you, so you must not give him room for an opening to come into your heart or your mind. Your mind must be My mind. Your thoughts must be My thoughts. Your truth must be My truth. Your spirit must be My Spirit."

"If your right eye causes you to sin, pluck it out and cast it from you; for it is more profitable for you that one of your members perish, than for your whole body to be cast into hell." Matthew 5:29

God says, "Satan is a manipulator of the mind. He sneaks in the door of your mind and manipulates your thoughts to war against the mind of Christ in you. The enemy can war against everything in you that is not renewed."

"So [it was] during supper, Satan having already put the thought of betraying Jesus in the heart of Judas Ischariot..." John 13:2 (AMP)

June 30

God says, "You're to say to all the satanic thoughts coming into your mind or trying to inundate you, 'Get behind me for it is written. It's written in the tablets of my heart, and God has put *rhema* principles there, and I'm going to speak them and be true to them.'"

"Let not mercy and truth forsake you; bind them around your neck, write them on the tablet of your heart." Proverbs 3:3

"You are clearly an epistle of Christ...written not with ink but by the Spirit of the living God, not on tablets of stone but on tablets of flesh, that is, of the heart." 2 Corinthians 3:3

God says, "The enemy has always corrupted My word. He hates My word. He hates My word growing you up. He hates My word, which makes your lips obedient and which words strengthen and cleanse you."

"For I know this, that after my departure savage wolves will come in among you, not sparing the flock. Also from among yourselves men will rise up, speaking perverse things, to draw away the disciples after themselves. Therefore watch..." Acts 20:29-31a

July 1

Satan's single purpose is to ruin the soul and spirit of man and separate him from God. He put it into the heart of Judas Ischariot to betray the Son of God, but Jesus Christ knew that He had come from God and was returning to God. (See John 13:2-3.)

> *"For we do not wrestle against flesh and blood, but... against the rulers of the darkness of this age, against spiritual hosts of wickedness in the heavenly places."* Ephesians 6:12

God says, "Who has come to kill and steal God's people, His purpose, His will, His very existence in the hearts of people who once walked with Him, who now do not walk with Him?"

> *"And the Lord said, 'Simon, Simon! Indeed, Satan has asked for you, that he may sift you as wheat. But I have prayed for you, that your faith should not fail; and when you have returned to Me, strengthen your brethren.'"*
> Luke 22:31-32

July 2

God says, "You cannot accept or compromise or give an ear of understanding to darkness because there is no understanding evil except that Satan is the author of it."

God says, "Do not go into the world and out of Christ."

"He was a murderer from the beginning, and does not stand in the truth, because there is no truth in him..." John 8:44b

God says, "You should cling to Me at all times, even when you're troubled, because troubling gives you an idea that the enemy is here. Despair is a mark of the enemy's foot tracks in the sand of life. Do not let him steal and put things in your heart that will break our relationship."

"The thief does not come except to steal, and to kill, and destroy. I have come that they may have life, and that they may have it more abun-dantly." John 10:10

July 3

God asks, "Though the enemy rails, do you think I believe him? Do you think I hear him? Do you think if I cannot hear the prayer of the unrighteous, how can I hear his railing accusations? Because he accuses you, does that mean I accept it?"

> *"But your iniquities have separated you from your God; and your sins have hidden His face from you, so that He will not hear."* Isaiah 59:2

> *"...for the accuser of our brethren, who accused them before our God day and night, has been cast down."* Revelation 12:10b

God says, "Do not give the enemy any place, because he walks about seeking whom he may devour. Are you fully determined that only My word counts? Only My way counts? Only My thoughts count?"

> *"...and he has no claim on Me. [He has nothing in common with Me; there is nothing in Me that belongs to him, and he has no power over Me.]"* John 14:30b (AMP)

July 4

God says, "The prince of darkness is at work. He's trying to delude, deceive, and grieve the hearts and torment the minds of those who will try to stay with the Lord. You must stand fast in the Lord and in the power of His might. You must execute His word. You must deliberate. You must meditate. You must have communion with the most holy God, for He said, 'Come.'"

> *"The coming of the lawless one is according to the working of Satan, with all power, signs, and lying wonders, and with all unrighteous deception among those who perish, because they did not receive the love of the truth, that they might be saved."* 2 Thessalonians 2:9-10

God says, "That's the purpose of the enemy saying, 'Has God said?' (See Genesis 3:1.) He is inferring by question, are you sure God is in this? Are you sure God does not want you to go this other way? Are you sure that this is of the Spirit?"

> *"Then many false prophets will rise up and deceive many. And because lawlessness will abound, the love of many will grow cold. But he who endures to the end shall be saved."*
> Matthew 24:11-13

July 5

God says, "For I say unto all those who labor in the flesh, you have to end the labor because My Spirit is not quickened by flesh, nor quickens flesh. My Spirit is a quickening spirit, and spirit is the movement of My energy found nowhere else. Except one is in the spirit, he cannot divide the darkness from the light. There is darkness in his own flesh, light in his own spirit. Flesh cannot know spirit nor spirit flesh. These two are set against each other, and it's time for Me to declare an end to flesh."

"Now this I say, brethren, that flesh and blood cannot inherit the kingdom of God; nor does corruption inherit incorruption."
1 Corinthians 15:50

God says, "The enemy plants furrows in the undeveloped mind and body of his own defiled nature, and I plant the good seed in good soil of the spirit realm. For I do not sow seed in the flesh realm, nor do I expect to reap from that realm. The flesh is trying to understand Me, but it cannot, nor will it ever. What's born of flesh is flesh, and what's born of Spirit is spirit. One cannot prosper. Another will never fail."

July 6

God says, "You should flee from the enemy if you're too weak to resist."

> *"...beware lest you also fall from your own steadfastness, being led away with the error of the wicked."* 2 Peter 3:17b

God says, "When you see the storm clouds rise and come against you and come over your dwelling, know you well that I, the Lord your God, have called you to be secure. I have called you to be a strong pillar, not to waver, not to be afraid. For there is nothing to fear, saith the Lord, but fear. I would not have you to be afraid of anything. I would not have you take on a spirit of fear or even be concerned. Don't be anxious. My covenant of peace is upon you."

> *"For the mountains shall depart and hills be removed, but My kindness shall not depart from you, nor shall My covenant of peace be removed, says the Lord, who has mercy on you."* Isaiah 54:10

July 7

God says, "The devil can't make you do it. He can only show you temptation of the evil one. Fasting and 'thus saith the Lord' are effective weapons against temptation."

"Then Jesus was led up by the Spirit into the wilderness to be tempted by the devil. And when He had fasted forty days and forty nights...the tempter came to Him, and he said, 'If you are the Son of God, command that these stones become bread.' But Jesus answered and said, 'It is written, man shall not live by bread alone, but by every word that proceeds from the mouth of God.'" Matthew 4:1-4

God says, "The enemy is about his evil work, and the earth is growing darker and darker. So, rise up and be a mighty army for Me, like Gideon, and be about your Father's business, for I am Lord over your earth. I am the Lord who is going to send My Son, and the evil will be over in one moment when He comes. Be ready. The tribulation is on, and it's coming. Get ready, and know that I will receive those who will let Me protect them and seal them by My angelic army. They'll be sealed on the forehead, that they will not be hurt by the coming that is to come, and you'll be hidden away in the wilderness."

July 8

God says, "When you're so comfortable in your Christian walk, you must realize that that's the time when the enemy will strike most. Be alert."

"Accordingly then, let us not sleep, as the rest do, but let us keep wide awake (alert, watchful, cautious, and on our guard) and let us be sober (calm, collected, and circumspect)."
1 Thessalonians 5:6 (AMP)

God says, "Because the enemy comes, you must come unto Me, that I might give you rest. Because he comes, you must come unto Me in the spirit of revelation."

"...if anyone desires to come after Me, let him deny himself, and take up his cross daily, and follow Me." Luke 9:23

"...if anyone thirsts, let him come to Me and drink." John 7:37

July 9

God asks, "Do you think the enemy is stronger than My word? Do you think the power of his words are stronger than My word? I want to tell you that he's terrified by My words if they are spoken in spirit and truth—spoken from your spirit with a revelation conviction that you are able to do battle with him successfully."

"And the Lord said to Satan, 'The Lord rebuke you, Satan! The Lord who has chosen Jerusalem rebuke you!...'" Zechariah 3:2

"Then Jesus said to him, 'Away with you, Satan! For it is written...'" Matthew 4:10

God says, "Even the demonic powers recognize My strength. They're still before My word, cringing. If they, the powers of darkness, can cringe, you should submit, surrender, and declare Christ in you, your hope of glory."

"You believe that there is one God. You do well. Even the demons believe—and tremble!" James 2:19

July 10

God says, "In this hour you have more demonic attacks upon Christians than any other hour. In this hour you have more potentiality for greatness than any other hour. There are few who are rising up to the pinnacle of spiritual maturity, who are speaking the truth in love, speaking to a dying world that they must acknowledge that Jesus Christ is Lord, to the glory of God."

> *"And the dragon was enraged with the woman,*
> *and he went to make war with the rest of her*
> *offspring, who keep the commandments of God*
> *and have the testimony of Jesus Christ."*
> Revelation 12:17

God asks, "Do you have the power today to eliminate the enemy from under your feet? Are you able to trod upon the serpent's head in the trials that you're going through? Are you able to walk over them and not be walked on by them? Can you say, 'Devil, leave me'? Can you say, 'Satan, get behind me'? Can you say it, trusting Me with all your heart, mind, soul, and strength?"

> *"You have made him to have dominion over the*
> *works of Your hands; You have put all things*
> *under his feet."* Psalm 8:6

July 11

God says, "Man must count the cost before he goes to war. If you war in the flesh, it will be futile. If you war against the flesh, it will be futile. If you engage in any activity with flesh, it will cause unrest within you, and it will take the peace and joy from you."

"For the weapons of our warfare are not carnal but mighty in God for pulling down strong-holds." 2 Corinthians 10:4

God says, "Be on the alert and be at war, for the war is at hand, and warfare must be done. There must be more prayer, more fasting, more believing, more travail for you to come above the thickening cloud of evil."

"Watch, stand fast in the faith, be brave, be strong." 1 Corinthians 16:13

"Because you have kept My command to perse-vere, I also will keep you from the hour of trial which shall come upon the whole world, to test those who dwell on the earth." Revelation 3:10

July 12

God says, "Christ Jesus, My Son, came and destroyed the works of the enemy. In other words, He destroyed the ability of the enemy to have preeminence over you. If My Spirit is not able to do it, then who can do it? If God cannot overcome the enemy, then why worship Me? Are you convinced I'm who I say I am, I'm able to do all things, and with God all things are possible, nothing is impossible?"

> *"Who is he who overcomes the world, but he who believes that Jesus is the Son of God?"*
> 1 John 5:5

> *"For with God nothing is ever impossible and no word from God shall be without power or impossible of fulfillment."* Luke 1:37 (AMP)

God says, "When you submit to God, you don't have to resist the devil."

> *"Leave no [such] room or foothold for the devil [give no opportunity to him]."* Ephesians 4:27 (AMP)

Submission to God closes the door of opportunity to the enemy.

July 13

God says, "I see no defeat for the children of God. When I look to the end, I do not see the enemy raise his hands in victory. I see the enemy being thrown in the lake of fire."

"Then He will also say to those on the left hand, 'Depart from Me, you cursed, into the everlasting fire prepared for the devil and his angels.'" Matthew 25:41

God says, "My spiritual reality for your physical reality will break the powers of defeat in your lives."

"For assuredly, I say to you, whoever says to this mountain, 'Be removed and be cast into the sea,' and does not doubt in his heart, but believes those things he says will come to pass, he will have whatever he says. Therefore I say to you, whatever things you ask when you pray, believe that you receive them, and you will have them." Mark 11:23-24

July 14

God says, "Go forth and break out into joy, the very nature that will effectively discourage the enemy when he knows you are not afraid, and you are not yielding. Walk in assurance, and walk in the manner in which the enemy will know that you know his devices, and you are not impressed. Assume the posture of the victor."

> *"Then David said to Goliath, 'You come to me with a sword, a spear, and with a javelin. But I come to you in the name of the Lord of hosts...whom you have taunted. This day the Lord will deliver you up into my hands...'"*
> 1 Samuel 17:45-46a (NASB)

God says, "When you enter your homes, enter with a shout and drive the demons out. Shout for joy and take possession of your homes, even when there are others being carnally minded. Drive those demons out before you sit down to your meal. Stand and shout and praise the Lord before you taste the food. Oh, My people, there's a banqueting table I've set before you. Taste of that."

> *"...all the people shall shout with a great shout; then the wall of the city will fall down flat..."*
> Joshua 6:5

July 15

God says, "Let Me be the chief bishop of your souls. Let Me silence the enemy. Let Me put him to route through My Spirit within you. Let the spirit within you react as though you had already conquered the enemy. Let your spirit know it is finished."

"For the word of the Lord is right, and all His work is done in truth." Psalm 33:4

God says, "But I have come to make you glad that I have power greater than he, and I am able to destroy everything he raised in your face if you are in Me, and I am in you."

"...for this purpose the Son of God was manifested, that He might destroy the works of the devil." 1 John 3:8b

July 16

God says, "Do not give the enemy a foothold, a place of influence in your life. Stand your ground, and face the enemy of your soul, and do battle with him, and put him under your feet."

"Then Jesus said to him, 'Away with you, Satan! For it is written, you shall worship the Lord your God, and Him only you shall serve.' Then the devil left Him, and behold, angels came and ministered to Him." Matthew 4:10-11

God says, "You don't have to flee from the enemy. Instead, you are to make a wall around the mind that he can't penetrate, by thinking on those things that make for peace."

"My son, keep my words, and treasure my commands within you. Keep my commands and live, and my law as the apple of your eye. Bind them on your fingers; write them on the tablet of your heart." Proverbs 7:1-3

July 17

God says, "You must learn how to still your mind, thoughts, and emotions, and come to an end of yourselves, that you might come to the beginning of learning how to be spirit as well as truth. Let mental exercise cease, and let the spirit take charge."

God says, "We are to sit under God's Spirit and learn sweet communion with Him. Spirit only can understand spiritual truth."

> *"So that you incline your ear to wisdom, and apply your heart to understanding; yes, if you cry out for discernment, and lift up your voice for understanding, then you will understand the fear of the Lord, and find the knowedge of God."* Proverbs 2:2-3,5

God says, "In taking your rest, do not be noisy within your mind. Learn how to subdue your mind by the Spirit's power. Recognize who you will and can be if you but let self go, if you but surrender the thoughts of your mind to the mind of Christ."

> *"And be constantly renewed in the spirit of your mind [having a fresh mental and spiritual attitude]."* Ephesians 4:23 (AMP)

July 18

God asks, "What is the higher goal—to be an intellectual giant or a spiritual genius?"

The intellectual mind is knowledge of men. The spiritual mind is knowledge of God.

> *"The reverent and worshipful fear of the Lord is the beginning (the chief and choice part) of Wisdom, and the knowledge of the Holy One is insight and understanding."* Proverbs 9:10 (AMP)

God asks, "Well then, do you think it is impossible to think spiritually?"

God says we are spirits, and if we are spirits, it is possible to think spiritually.

> *"These things we also speak, not in words which man's wisdom teaches but which the Holy Spirit teaches, comparing spiritual things with spiritual."* 1 Corinthians 2:13

July 19

God says, "You can't understand Christ in your mind. Your mind isn't big enough to comprehend Him, but your heart is big enough to grasp Christ and make Him your own."

"But if from there you will seek...the Lord your God, you will find Him if you [truly] seek Him with all your heart [and mind] and soul and life." Deuteronomy 4:29 (AMP)

God says, "I want above all things, My unity to come. You must be willing to be delivered from your self purpose, your self inclination, and be delivered into a godly inclination that will exclude your own reasoning and logic that you know what to do. You do not know what to do. Without Me you can do nothing."

"I am the vine, you are the branches. He who abides in Me, and I in him, bears much fruit; for without Me you can do nothing." John 15:5

July 20

God says, "Understanding by My Spirit is far greater than the truth you understand with your small degree of maturity. Let the mind be dead unto the life of the Spirit."

> *"Now the mind of the flesh [which is sense and reason without the Holy Spirit] is death... but the mind of the [Holy] Spirit is life and [soul] peace..."* Romans 8:6 (AMP)

God says, "You had better let your heart become pitted against your mind and kill the mind if necessary, until it cannot work contrary to My will in your heart. Your own understanding is known by the evil one."

> *"For this reason we also, since the day we heard it, do not cease to pray for you, and to ask that you may be filled with the knowledge of His will in all wisdom and spiritual understanding."*
> Colossians 1:9

July 21

God says, "You are abusing your own heart when your mind is at work. When your mind is set on your own will, you cannot do anything but abuse yourself. My will should make your will die. Let the enemy know that he cannot touch you again because your will and your flesh are crucified."

"And He said, 'Abba, Father, all things are possible for You. Take this cup away from Me; nevertheless, not what I will, but what You will.'" Mark 14:36

God says, "You must be aware that the enemy will try to subvert the heart by feeding it from the mind things that you take in by degree or passivity, allowing the mind to contaminate the heart."

"Because the carnal mind is enmity against God; for it is not subject to the law of God, nor indeed can be." Romans 8:7

"Let this mind be in you which was also in Christ Jesus." Philippians 2:5

July 22

The mind of God demands complete honesty.

"For we take thought beforehand and aim to be honest and absolutely above suspicion, not only in the sight of the Lord but also in the sight of men." 2 Corinthians 8:21 (AMP)

God says, "You need to bathe your minds in the waters of My word so that your words and your thoughts become pleasing in My sight."

"Let the words of my mouth and the meditation of my heart be acceptable in Your sight, O Lord, my strength and my redeemer."
Psalm 19:14

July 23

God says, "And your mind must think on whatever is pure, whatever is virtuous, whatever is good, whatever has good report, the pure—think on these things; and so you are to use your mind under the governing of the Spirit."

"Set your mind on things above, not on things on the earth." Colossians 3:2

God says, "The soul is joined to the heart-mind complex, and the soul derives its pleasure from thinking on things that are pure, good, and holy, that have virtue and good report."

"My son, pay attention to my wisdom; lend your ear to my understanding, that you may preserve discretion, and your lips may keep knowledge."
Proverbs 5:1-2

"My soul longs, yes, even faints for the courts of the Lord; my heart and my flesh cry out for the living God." Psalm 84:2

July 24

God says, "The greatest hindrance in the walk of a believer is not the devil. It's the way you think."

"For as he thinks in his heart, so is he..."
Proverbs 23:7a

"I the Lord search the mind, I try the heart, even to give to every man according to his ways, according to the fruit of his doings."
Jeremiah 17:10 (AMP)

God says, "Don't believe in your own reality. How long will you let your mind rule your reality? I tell you, stop the endless strife of your flesh with My Spirit. Release yourself and surrender to Me now. Are you still saying, 'I cannot. I'm too used to my old way'? Well, have your own way, but I'll have a new way with My people."

"All the ways of a man are pure in his own eyes, but the Lord weighs the spirits. Commit your works to the Lord, and your thoughts will be established." Proverbs 16:2-3

July 25

God says, "You must come before Him in your spiritual image. You do not come to Him in your body. You come to Him in your spirit, leaving mind and body behind, if necessary, in order to know Him and the power of His resurrection. Life is not in you because the body is alive. Life is not in you because the mind is alive. Life is in you because I am alive in the body and the mind and the spirit."

"And if Christ is in you, the body is dead because of sin, but the spirit is life because of righteousness." Romans 8:10

God says, "Let that sudden boredom that's in your minds be bound by the Spirit of God. That can free you to exercise your liberty in the Spirit, and rise up, and enjoy the beauty of being a spiritual man or woman of God. Don't be indifferent to Me, My children. I see it all the time on this earth, and there are so many that can take Me or leave Me."

"In the multitude of my [anxious] thoughts within me, Your comforts cheer and delight my soul!" Psalm 94:19 (AMP)

July 26

God says, "A double-minded man has a double mind, a mind that receives the revelation of the natural man and the revelation of God, and these two cannot mix, and these two bring a division of the soul and the spirit. The man that is not living harmoniously with his spirit and his soul joined together is a man who is not able to live in harmony with the Spirit of God."

> *"Hear, my son, and receive my sayings, and the years of your life will be many. I have taught you in the way of wisdom; I have led you in right paths. When you walk, your steps will not be hindered, and when you run, you will not stumble. Take firm hold of instruction, do not let go; keep her, for she is your life."*
> Proverbs 4:10-13

You are not what you think you are. What you think, you are.

God says, "Thinking cannot listen."

July 27

God says, "You must be aware that you must take spiritual inventory that asks:

1. Lord, what have I done to miss the mark in my life at this time?
2. What steps need I take to return to my first love?
3. Wherein have I thought in my heart things that aren't born of You?"

"The Lord is near to those who have a broken heart, and saves such as have a contrite spirit."
Psalm 34:18

God says, "Flesh is the limitation upon a man's spiritual nature set upon him by reason of his accepting a limited life in the Spirit."

July 28

God asks, "Are you willing to allow Me to invade your character and conduct with My truth? Are you willing to exchange your nature for Mine?"

> *"Search me, O God, and know my heart; try me, and know my anxieties; and see if there is any wicked way in me, and lead me in the way everlasting."* Psalm 139:23-24

Change my heart, O God. I am yours totally. Take off the vestiges of my old ways, and make me pure before you, oh holy God.

> *"As for me, I will see Your face in righteousness; I shall be satisfied when I awake in Your likeness."* Psalm 17:15

July 29

God says, "You have no ignorance, for there is no ignorance in those who are taught well; and you've been taught well through the years to examine yourself whether you be in the faith."

"Examine and test and evaluate your own selves to see whether you are holding to your faith and showing the proper fruits of it. Test and prove yourselves [not Christ]..." 2 Corinthians 13:5a (AMP)

God says, "I have made it abundantly clear that you are to crucify your flesh with its affections and lusts. What are the affections and lusts of the flesh, My children? The affections and lusts of the flesh are those things that are your treasure. Where man's treasure is, is his heart. If you see that you gravitate to these things of the flesh, that is where your treasure is."

"So is he who lays up treasure for himself, and is not rich toward God." Luke 12:21

July 30

God says, "You cannot live in Me and let the world live in you. You cannot live in the world and have the Father live in you. You cannot revisit Egypt and be in Canaan, nor can you visit Canaan and be in Egypt. There is one or the other. Choose you this day whom and what you will serve."

"For all people walk each in the name of his god, but we will walk in the name of the Lord our God, forever and ever." Micah 4:5

God says, "My Son must be in all that you do. My Son must be reflected from your lives. Examine My Son, examine His characteristics, examine His nature, and then show that nature, and compare it with the nature that you have. Do you not know that you have a long way to go?"

"Whoever says he abides in Him ought [as a personal debt] to walk and conduct himself in the same way in which He walked and conducted Himself." 1 John 2:6 (AMP)

July 31

God asks, "Are you prepared to obey what I have said? Are you coming to My word with the intention of letting it change you? Those who hunger and thirst after Me shall be filled with Me. Knock, and I stand ready to open the door to newness in Me." (See Matthew 5:8.)

> *"Keep on asking and it will be given you; keep on seeking and you will find; keep on knocking [reverently] and [the door] will be opened to you."* Matthew 7:7 (AMP)

Knowledge of the truth should create responsibility within us. In God's word, knowledge without obedience is sin.

> *"Therefore, to him who knows to do good and does not do it, to him it is sin."* James 4:17

August 1

To know and not to do is to sin. (See James 4:17.)

Christ said to His disciples, "Why do you call Me 'Lord, Lord' and do not do what I say?" He is telling you to either stop calling Him Lord or start obeying His word to you.

> *"But why do you call Me 'Lord, Lord,' and not do the things which I say?"* Luke 6:46

Do we demand that God tell us more and more about Him, when we've not obeyed what He has said before? God encourages us to make a decision to go all the way with Him.

> *"Jesus answered and said to him, 'If anyone loves Me, he will keep My word; and My Father will love him, and We will come to him and make Our home with him. He who does not love Me does not keep My words; and the word which you hear is not Mine but the Father's who sent Me.'"* John 14:23-24

August 2

Asking is a necessary step, but it is obedience to your Lord that humbles the heart.

"Oh, that they had such a heart in them that they would fear Me and always keep all My commandments, that it might be well with them and with their children forever." Deuteronomy 5:29

God says, "My Son will come, and it will be in a time when you least expect Me. But I am coming, so endure and occupy till I come; but stand in the way of the Lord's word. Stand in humbleness, and fall on your face before My mighty presence, for My angels are around you. My presence is in you, and I've sent My Son's Spirit to reside on this earth."

"So He said, 'No, but as Commander of the army of the Lord I have now come.' And Joshua fell on his face to the earth, and worshiped and said to Him, 'What does my Lord say to His servant?'" Joshua 5:14

August 3

God says, "To obey is courage; to disobey is cowardice."

" '...our God whom we serve is able to deliver us from the burning fiery furnace, and He will deliver us from your hand, O king. But if not, let it be known to you...that we do not serve your gods, nor will we worship the gold image which you have set up.' Then King Nebuchadnezzar was astonished...and spoke...'Did we not cast three men bound into the midst of the fire?' '...Look!' he answered, 'I see four men loose, walking in the midst of the fire...and the form of the fourth is like the Son of God.'" Daniel 3:17-18, 24-25

God says, "My Son did stand in the valley. My Son walked in the valley. My Son slept in the valley. My Son learned of Me in the valley. My Son was taught in the valley. My Son grew strength in the valley. I say unto you this day, choose My way. It is narrow, but it leads to life. It is the only way. Do not stray."

August 4

"As for me and my house, we shall serve the Lord" means we will believe and obey the word of God.

" '...choose for yourselves this day whom you will serve...but as for me and my house, we will serve the Lord.' And the people said to Joshua, 'The Lord our God we will serve, and His voice we will obey!'" Joshua 24:15,24

God says, "The reason Enoch walked with God, and he was not, was because he walked with God in the word for every area of his being. He simply decided to be what I wanted him to be."

"By faith Enoch was translated so that he did not see death, 'and was not found because God had translated him'; for before his translation he had this testimony, that he pleased God."
Hebrews 11:5

August 5

God says, "I want you to know more of how to follow and less of how to lead. I want you to know more of how to let Me rule before you try to take the rule. Do not lead your Shepherd, your Chief Bishop of your soul, your Christ, for He must lead you."

> *"...these are the ones who follow the Lamb wherever He goes. These were redeemed from among men, being firstfruits to God and to the Lamb."*
> Revelation 14:4b

God says, "Do not be heavily burdened by My words, for the obedience to these words will set you free. Remember the secret of My Son and of the apostles was in their obedience, and was in the purity that came from the obedience."

> *"For as by one man's disobedience many were made sinners, so also by one Man's obedience many will be made righteous."* Romans 5:19

> *"Having confidence in your obedience...knowing that you will do even more than I say."*
> Philemon 21

August 6

God says, "If I'm not Lord of all, I'm not Lord at all; and I must be Lord of all the kingdoms of your heart. Who occupies the majority of your life each week? Who occupies your thought life? What motivates your very actions and behavior? Who are you? As Christ would be? Who are you in love? As Christ would be? Who are you in every aspect of your life? As Christ would be?"

> *"You alone are the Lord; You have made*
> *heaven, the heaven of heavens, with all their*
> *host, the earth and all things on it, the seas and*
> *all that is in them. And You preserve them all.*
> *The host of heaven worships You."* Nehemiah 9:6

Do we ever say that we can't exercise the standard of righteousness because little ones can't obey it?

God says, "If My Spirit dwells in you, no matter what the age, you can obey Me. You can obey."

> *"Then the boy Samuel ministered to the*
> *Lord...the Lord came and stood and called as at*
> *other times, 'Samuel! Samuel!' And Samuel*
> *answered, 'Speak, for your servant hears.'"*
> 1 Samuel 3:1a, 10

August 7

God says, "You can't be ambivalent and double-minded and receive My full blessing. Every time you say no to Me it is more difficult to say yes. Do not keep My ministry of Christ at bay in your life."

"No servant can serve two masters; for either he will hate the one and love the other, or else he will be loyal to the one and despise the other. You cannot serve God and mammon." Luke 16:13

"He is a double-minded man, unstable in all his ways." James 1:8

God asks, "Are you willing to be changed, My people? Are you willing to be filled, My people? Are you willing to be corrected, My people? Will you be disciplined by Me because discipleship means discipline."

"If you are willing and obedient, you shall eat the good of the land;" Isaiah 1:19

"Then everyone came whose heart was stirred, and everyone whose spirit was willing..."
Exodus 35:21a

Are you willing to be made willing?

August 8

God says, "I can invite you to this truth or that truth, or this principle or that principle, or this walk or that walk. I can invite you to just lay all aside, except your priority to be in Me. But you must have a willing spirit."

"So when Jesus heard these things, He said to him, 'You still lack one thing. Sell all that you have and distribute to the poor, and you will have treasure in heaven; and come, follow Me.' But when he heard this, he became very sorrowful, for he was very rich." Luke 18:22-23

God says, "Dismiss imaginations in obedience to the word of God."

"Casting down arguments and every high thing that exalts itself against the knowledge of God, bringing every thought into captivity to the obedience of Christ." 2 Corinthians 10:5

"And so it may not happen, when he hears the words of this curse, that he blesses himself in his heart, saying, 'I shall have peace, even though I walk in the imagination of my heart'—as though the drunkard could be included with the sober." Deuteronomy 29:19

August 9

God says, "Unless I say, unless I'm Lord over that decision, then you have vacated your seat of responsibility and obedience to submit to My word before you act on your own."

King Hezekiah foolishly exposed all of Judah's wealth to Babylon. Scripture says that there was nothing in his house or in all his dominion that Hezekiah did not show them. Judgment was pronounced by the Lord because Hezekiah leaned to his own understanding and did not seek God. All was carried to Babylon. (See 2 Kings 20:12-19.)

God says, "You don't need to defend yourselves. You need to uphold Me. You don't need to please others. You need to please Me, because if you please Me, and they are truly Mine, they'll be pleased by your pleasing Me, not them. Stop pleasing men."

"But as we have been approved by God to be entrusted with the gospel, even so we speak, not as pleasing men, but God who tests our hearts."
1 Thessalonians 2:4

August 10

Jesus Christ is the will of the Father.

"In the beginning was the Word, and the Word was with God, and the Word was God. And the Word became flesh and dwelt among us...."
John 1:1,14

"But whoever keeps His word, truly the love of God is perfected in him. By this we know that we are in Him. He who says he abides in Him ought himself also to walk just as He walked."
1 John 2:5-6

God says, "Until Christ is fully formed in you, you are still groping in half-light. When you insist on walking away from the light, you can only go into darkness." (See Galatians 4:19.)

"...God is light and in Him is no darkness at all. If we say that we have fellowship with Him, and walk in darkness, we lie and do not practice the truth. But if we walk in the light as He is in the light...the blood of Jesus Christ His Son cleanses us from all sin." 1 John 1:5b-7

August 11

God says, "Forsake all, and trust Me!"

"...nevertheless I am not ashamed, for I know whom I have believed and am persuaded that He is able to keep what I have committed to Him until that day." 2 Timothy 1:12

"I have been young, and now am old; yet I have not seen the righteous forsaken..." Psalm 37:25a

God says, "You, My children, must trust in Me to such a total extent that you will never give place to the devil. It is a lack of trust in Me that brings the conditions for the entrance of your adversary."

"Casting all your care upon Him, for He cares for you." 1 Peter 5:7

"Cast your burden on the Lord, and He shall sustain you..." Psalm 55:22a

August 12

God says, "Trust the One who will never put conditions on His love for you. Trust the One who never willed for you to suffer or be hurt. Trust Me, because I will deliver you, saith the Lord. Trust Me. Do not trust yourself but trust Me."

"Who is among you who [reverently] fears the Lord, who obeys the voice of His servant, yet who walks in darkness and deep trouble and has no shining splendor [in his heart]? Let him rely on, trust in, and be confident in the name of the Lord, and let him lean upon and be supported by his God." Isaiah 50:10 (AMP)

God says, "In Jesus, My Son, you can trust what He says. You can trust what He did. You can trust who He is. You can trust what He is, for He is to you all things, if you but believe Him and trust Him with all your heart, for He is a God who honors faith."

"...Jesus answered, 'You say rightly that I am a king. For this cause I was born, and for this cause I have come into the world, that I should bear witness to the truth. Everyone who is of the truth hears My voice.'" John 18:37

August 13

God says, "Learn, My people, of Me, not of men, because who has failed you—God or man? Who has deserted you in time of need but God or man? I've never left you. Until the end of the age I will be with you and never forsake you."

"For He [God] Himself has said, I will not in any way fail you nor give you up nor leave you without support. [I will] not, [I will] not, [I will] not in any degree leave you helpless nor forsake nor let [you] down (relax My hold on you)! [Assuredly not!]" Hebrews 13:5b (AMP)

God says, "Stand with Me. Stand with Me. I am your lifeline. I am your lifeline today, and I am your lifeline every moment. I will never leave you nor forsake you. I will come for you again. Be sure I am coming, saith the Lord."

"I will not leave you orphans; I will come to you." John 14:18

August 14

God asks, "Do you believe in the highest standard that God has His children live in, or do you believe in a standard of the world?"

"So shall they fear the name of the Lord from the west, and His glory from the rising of the sun; When the enemy comes in like a flood, the Spirit of the Lord will lift up a standard against him." Isaiah 59:19

God says, "Go on while there is time. Do not stop. Go, as though you're climbing Mount Everest, and then another Everest, another Everest, and another Everest beyond that. Go without any doubt that you will make it."

"If you have run with the footmen, and they have wearied you, then how can you contend with horses? And if in the land of peace, in which you trusted, they wearied you, then how will you do in the floodplain of the Jordan?"
Jeremiah 12:5

August 15

God says, "As you go on in maturity, your choices are limited. You should be glad in that. You cannot have your way and expect Me to have My way on the road to spiritual maturity."

"When I was a child, I understood as a child, I thought as a child; but when I became a man, I put away childish things." 1 Corinthians 13:11

God says, "You will feel so secure in Me as your growth in Me continues. You'll come to the point where nothing can turn you to the right or to the left by the will of the enemy."

"Ponder the path of your feet, and let all your ways be established. Do not turn to the right or the left; remove your foot from evil."
Proverbs 4:26-27

August 16

God says, "It's never too late, My people, to go back to the foundational principles of your first love, and let it be taught by Me. Remember, you've forfeited the right to be yours when you became Mine."

> *" 'Now, therefore,' says the Lord, 'Turn to Me with all your heart, with fasting, with weeping, and with mourning.' So rend your heart, and not your garments; return to the Lord your God, for He is gracious and merciful, slow to anger, and of great kindness..."* Joel 2:12-13

God says, "I accepted you willingly in My kingdom, and you came in the way you were, and I accepted you just as you were, but that doesn't mean I am glad to have you remain as you were."

> *"Therefore, laying aside all malice, all deceit, hypocrisy, envy, and all evil speaking, as newborn babes, desire the pure milk of the word, that they may grow thereby, if indeed you have tasted that the Lord is gracious."* 1 Peter 2:1-3

August 17

God says, "Do not be satisfied with where you are. Do not be anxious, but do not be satisfied, and don't think within yourselves that you have achieved much when there is much yet to be achieved. What you have achieved is only a beginning."

"...leaving the discussion of the elementary principles of Christ, let us go on to perfection, not laying again the foundation of repentance from dead works and of faith toward God, of the doctrine of baptisms, of laying on of hands, of resurrection of the dead, and of eternal judgment." Hebrews 6:1-2

God says, "I want you to know that I know your concerns and the desires of your heart. I will only do what people will allow Me to do with their will. If they allow Me to be strong in their lives, I will be strong. If they will for Me to not be there, then I will not force Myself upon anyone. I will not go where I am not wanted, because I love you, My children. I will not force Myself upon you, but I want you to live by My word."

"He who receives you receives Me, and he who receives Me receives Him who sent Me."
Matthew 10:40

August 18

God says, "There are those upon this earth now who are growing into full-grown trees planted by the rivers of water of the word, having been washed by the washing of the word. And having been reformed, and renewed, and renovated, they are becoming My grown ones, tall spiritually, strong spiritually, able spiritually, Mine spiritually, and going on through the eternity of eternities to become like I am, as I said through My Son."

"Though your beginning was small, yet your latter end would increase abundantly." Job 8:7

God says, "I am beginning to do a new thing in each heart who has any hunger for Me. I will be there. I will never leave you nor forsake you, as long as you seek Me early and seek Me late. I am your Lord. I am the God of the inward man. I am the God of the spirit and the God of the soul and heart. I am the God of gods and the Lord of lords, when My Lordship is fully capable of consuming you, and you realize that you are nothing without Me, that your very breath is sustained by Me."

August 19

God says, "Make a covenant of love with Me that you will let Me grow you up quickly, for the time is short."

"Now therefore, if you will indeed obey My voice and keep My covenant, then you shall be a special treasure to Me above all people; for all the earth is Mine. And you shall be to Me a kingdom of priests and a holy nation."
Exodus 19:5-6a

God says He has far greater adventure for us in the spirit than anything the world can ever offer us. The Holy Spirit says do not go for the allure of the world's adventures to go here and there. God wants you to experience the greatness of God.

Take God's word to heart now. Return to your first love.

"That we who first trusted in Christ should be to the praise of His glory." Ephesians 1:12

August 20

Do we see the growth of God's character and nature in us? Is He bigger than He was a few days, a week, a month ago? Are we allowing Him to grow us up in Christ?

> *"[For my determined purpose is] that I may know Him [that I may progressively become more deeply and intimately acquainted with Him...]"* Philippians 3:10a (AMP)

God says if we don't take our growth in Him seriously, one day we will say, "Oh Lord, had I only known, I'd have done what You said."

God says, "Don't you know? How many years have you walked this way? More than the disciples had a chance to walk with their Lord, you walked with the Lord's voice. The Shepherd has always spoken, and when He speaks, your responsibility is to say, 'Yes, Lord, and amen, so be it.'"

Then do it!

August 21

God says, "So many of My children have started in things of the Spirit, and they've been excited, and they've been caught up in a whirlwind of activities and excitement and anticipation; and then they have turned because they were not grounded in My word."

> *"And that from childhood you have known the Holy Scriptures, which are able to make you wise for salvation through faith which is in Christ Jesus...that the man of God may be complete, thoroughly equipped for every good work."* 2 Timothy 3:15,17

God says, "You must be able to, by faith, begin to say what I say about your situation. What does God say? God says think the best. He believes the best, and love never fails if it's My one hundred percent agape love. Whatever is not of self is the nature of your spiritual growth that I will encourage to continue."

> (Love) *"bears all things, believes all things, hopes all things, endures all things. Love never fails..."* 1 Corinthians 13:7-8a

Grow on! Grow on! Grow on!

August 22

God says, "What will throw this earth into chaos quicker than any other thing will be the multiplication of untruth. Evil is the denial of truth. Untruth produces unhappiness; and when you are unhappy, you are unable to realize your potential in the Spirit."

"He shall pray to God, and He will delight in him, He shall see His face with joy, for He restores to man His righteousness." Job 33:26

God says, "Oh, you need to know what joy it is to seek your King, your coming King; for He will come in glory. He will not come as a humble one in a manger again. He will come in triumph, in power. He will render justice upon this earth. You need to look forward to that, because that's the hope that will hold My people together, the very fact of maranatha, Lord Jesus is coming."

August 23

God says, "A body is made of multifaceted members, and none is unneeded. Even the weaker members are most necessary as I've told you. Weaker simply means that the willingness is there, but they're not risen up yet."

"God gives power to the weak, and to those who have no might He increases strength."
Isaiah 40:29

God says, "When all members are functioning as they should function in their individual calling and corporate callings, then the personality of the church will become the personality of My Son."

"Till we all come to the unity of the faith and of the knowledge of the Son of God, to a perfect man, to the measure of the stature of the fullness of Christ; but, speaking the truth in love, may grow up in all things into Him who is the head—Christ—from whom the whole body, joined and knit together by what every joint supplies, according to the effective working by which every part does its share, causes growth of the body for the edifying of itself in love."
Ephesians 4:13, 15-16

August 24

God says, "Except your flesh be controlled by your heart and spirit, it's not controlled. It's out of control. It's rampant. It's tribulation for you."

"But I say, walk and live [habitually] in the [Holy] Spirit [responsive to and controlled and guided by the Spirit]; then you will certainly not gratify the cravings and desires of the flesh..."
Galatians 5:16 (AMP)

God says, "Declare war on yourself!"

"But I discipline my body and bring it into subjection, lest, when I have preached to others, I myself should become disqualified."
1 Corinthians 9:27

August 25

God says, "You weren't birthed from above to take one part, one-third of your nature, and discard the other two-thirds as though they did not count."

"Now may the God of peace Himself sanctify you completely; and may your whole spirit, soul, and body be preserved blameless at the coming of our Lord Jesus Christ." 1 Thessalonians 5:23

God says, "So, do not think that if you fix the outer man, the inner man will be fixed. If I see you discipline your outer man, your mind and body, then I will assist you in its perfection."

"But above all these things put on love, which is the bond of perfection. And let the peace of God rule in your hearts...and be thankful." Colossians 3:14-15

August 26

We are to quiet our impatient nature, to learn to relax and be still so that we can learn from God.

"My brethren, count it all joy when you fall into various trials, knowing that the testing of your faith produces patience. But let patience have its perfect work, that you may be perfect and complete, lacking nothing." James 1:2-4

God says, "Do not be hearers of the word only, but be ye doers of the word. Repent, My children, of those times I have tried to cut things from your life, those times when I have tried to tell you with gentle words, things you should get rid of, and things you should do to make yourslef more like Me."

"For we are His workmanship, created in Christ Jesus for good works, which God prepared beforehand that we should walk in them." Ephesians 2:10

August 27

God says, "Let go of your hold on yourself. Let Me take your place tonight. Let yourselves go, as if you were dying, for you are. The you is dying. The one I created before the foundation of the world is being birthed. Your flesh longs for control; your spirit needs My control."

"The Spirit of God has made me, and the breath of the Almighty gives me life." Job 33:4

God says, "Do not let your soulish nature seek to bind your spirit's freedom. Make no provision for the flesh."

"Stand fast therefore in the liberty by which Christ has made us free, and do not be entangled again with a yoke of bondage." Galatians 5:1

August 28

God says, "Rise today above the old, above your emotions, above the soulish nature, above your anger, above your turmoil, above your strife, above your anxiety, above your worry, above your depression, above all the old things that are not to be named among you."

"Knowing this, that our old man was crucified with Him, that the body of sin might be done away with, that we should no longer be slaves of sin. For he who has died has been freed from sin." Romans 6:6-7

God says, "Know no flesh. Let no flesh teach you anything, but only the spirit which is in a man that is directly in communion with God. For I, the Lord God, do not want you to be more appealing to Me in the flesh, but I want you to be quiet in the flesh and alive in your spirit."

"For he who sows to his flesh will of the flesh reap corruption, but he who sows to the Spirit will of the Spirit reap everlasting life." Galatians 6:8

August 29

God says, "Before Me, I shall strike down self. The self-nature will be burned in the fire of My return."

"But who can endure the day of His coming? And who can stand when He appears? For He is like a refiner's fire...He will sit as a refiner and a purifier of silver; He will purify the sons of Levi, and purge them as gold and silver, that we may offer to the Lord an offering in righteousness." Malachi 3:2-3

God says, "In all your ways, your priority, your time, your effort, your prayers, your intercession, your warfare, your meditation, your study, you are giving. My people are giving. They give of themselves, that I might be the only self that is real to them. If I'm not first, I'm nothing. I'm not Lord. I certainly do not control all your heart. I'm given a substance giving of your life, your time, your money, your effort. I'm only given a small portion of your very being. I want it all, because I own it all. I created it all. I made it all."

"Teach me to do Your will, for You are my God; Your Spirit is good. Lead me in the land of uprightness." Psalm 143:10

August 30

God says, "A born-again Christian should be under the Lordship of Jesus. They should constantly want to obey Him before they obey for any other reason. Reasoning is not My way except it be the reasoning of God. I do not always work in the ways of men, for I sometimes give instructions that are completely contrary to men's own thinking. I confound so their wisdom can be foolishness in this world, and My foolishness is their wisdom." (See 1 Corinthians 1:21,25.)

> *"And immediately, when Jesus perceived in His spirit that they reasoned thus within themselves, He said to them, 'Why do you reason about these things in your heart?'"* Mark 2:8

God says, "You will do what you want, either from your soulish nature or from your spiritual nature. The soulish nature will always find reason why I cannot, I cannot, I cannot."

> *"Now therefore, go, and I will be with your mouth and teach you what you shall say. But he said, 'O my Lord, please send by the hand of whomever else You may send.'"* Exodus 4:12-13

August 31

God says, "Be thankful today that you are where you are; and want to go further, for that was My desire for you to not be pleased with where you are. But until you receive the aim of Jesus Christ's will for you, you will not be where I want you to be. I am patient. I have forever. You do not. You are in mortality. You must seek to achieve that which I've set you on earth to do quickly that I may be pleased, and I may please you with My rewards. Be thankful today, My people."

"For thus says the Lord to the house of Israel; 'Seek Me and live.'" Amos 5:4

God says, "When the words that I speak become spirit and truth in you, they can turn your old nature away from interfering with the new nature."

"It is the Spirit who gives life; the flesh profits nothing. The words that I speak to you are spirit, and they are life." John 6:63

September 1

God says, "You may be carried up, oh sons, today, for there's nothing impeding you but your own self. When you learn to surrender and crucify that self, I will fill you fully with My self through My Christ."

> *"That Christ may dwell in your hearts through faith; that you, being rooted and grounded in love, may be able to comprehend with all the saints what is the width and length and depth and height—to know the love of Christ which passes knowledge; that you may be filled with all the fullness of God."* Ephesians 3:17-19

God says, "Instead of having done with lesser things, Satan would have you have done with the greater things of God. Instead of preparing your heart, your mind, your soul, your strength to serve the King of kings, you would be preparing your flesh to serve the king of flesh."

> *"Therefore, brethren, we are debtors—not to the flesh, to live according to the flesh. For if you live according to the flesh you will die; but if by the Spirit you put to death the deeds of the body, you will live."* Romans 8:12-13

September 2

God says, "I am challenging you this day to lay down your carnal life. Lay it down that it might die, and that it might no longer be a lesser thing that envelops you, and compels you, and controls you, and obsesses you. Begin to lay down the old and pick up the new."

"But put on the Lord Jesus Christ, and make no provision for the flesh, to fulfill its lusts."
Romans 13:14

God says, "Realize that when you cast that which you have withheld upon Me, I am able to cleanse all that part of your nature. When you cast it in finality, when you cast it with a fully persuaded heart that you do not want that in your nature, it will be gone. It will not return, and you will be blessed."

"And the Lord will deliver me from every evil work and preserve me for His heavenly kingdom..." 2 Timothy 4:18

September 3

God says, "You are to teach your bodies and your minds that you are not subject to their whims or to their wills. You are to teach your body and your mind that they are only accessories to who you are, spirit man; and that they will be subject in every moment to the direction of the Spirit."

"And whoever does not bear his cross and come after Me cannot be My disciple." Luke 14:27

God says, "When you put the body under subjection to the spirits and live, you are My reflection, and the word goes forth from you in a mighty way. But I want that to be the norm, not the exception, in your daily life. I want that to be the daily routine."

"For so the Lord has commanded us: 'I have set you as a light to the Gentiles, that you should be for salvation to the ends of the earth.'" Acts 13:47

September 4

God says, "This spiritual journey is a flight from the flesh. You have your cross of daily denial because exaltation of self keeps the body of Christ anemic and weak. When have you last denied your stubborn and carnal existences for a holy God? Remember, a carnal man is an enemy of God."

"...Do you not know that friendship with the world is enmity with God? Whoever therefore wants to be a friend of the world makes himself an enemy of God." James 4:4

God says, "Who stood beside My Son in the hall of Caiphas? Who was there praying with Him and willing to take His punishment? Are you willing to take Christ's punishment the world is dealing out to Him this day? His name is scorned, the Ten Commandments are scorned, the name of God is being removed from every edifice in the land and no one cries out. Say, 'As for me and my house, we will serve the Lord.'"

"You have not yet resisted to bloodshed, the striving against sin." Hebrews 12:4

September 5

God says, "When you invite Christ in you and believe in your heart and confess with your mouth, then He sojourns in spirit and truth with you to the extent you receive Him. I've called you to be one with Us. You have the choice, but it will cost you your very life. If you will deny yourself daily, take up your cross, and follow Me, you shall be one with Us."

"And he who does not take his cross and follow after Me is not worthy of Me. He who finds his life will lose it, and he who loses his life for My sake will find it." Matthew 10:38-39

God asks, "Who loves Me? Those who disregard their own nature to the point of letting it cease to exist in them, that My nature might become the Lord of their nature."

"But now having been set free from sin, and having become slaves of God, you have your fruit to holiness, and the end, everlasting life. For the wages of sin is death, but the gift of God is eternal life in Christ Jesus our Lord." Romans 6:22-23

September 6

God says, "You must want My Son, the Christ, more than you want life. You must want Him more than you want the world. You must want Him more than you want yourself. You must be selfless to find Him. You must give up your flesh in order to be crucified with Him, that He may rise from the ashes of your demise and occupy the fullness of your heart."

"But what things were gain to me, these I have counted loss for Christ. Yet indeed I also count all things loss for the excellence of the knowledge of Christ Jesus my Lord, for whom I have suffered the loss of all things, and count them as rubbish, that I may gain Christ." Philippians 3:7-8

God says, "Let Me take your place tonight. It will finally give you delight to know that I am in control, and you've lost control. You're not able to exercise any self. That's the final crucifixion."

"For we who live are always delivered to death for Jesus' sake, that the life of Jesus also may be manifested in our mortal flesh." 2 Corinthians 4:11

September 7

God says, "Do not lament the passing of yourself, for the expression of the new man in Me is that expression of perfection."

"And that you put on the new man which was created according to God, in righteousness and true holiness." Ephesians 4:24

"...that we may present every man perfect in Christ Jesus." Colossians 1:28b

God says, "Your spirit man has no trouble understanding, accepting, and bowing its knee to My word; for every knee shall bow and every tongue shall confess that I am Lord to the glory of God. And you shall have no problem when your soul man has no right to have any audience with your spirit except to fall upon its face and worship Me."

"That at the name of Jesus every knee should bow, of those in heaven, and of those on earth, and of those under the earth, and that every tongue should confess that Jesus Christ is Lord, to the glory of God the Father." Philippians 2:10-11

September 8

Issac, the son of promise, was telling his father that if he had to sacrifice him, sacrifice him to the Lord, not to the world. When have we laid our children on the altar like Abraham did with Issac? God says to sacrifice their flesh, not their spirit.

(And the Angel of the Lord said to Abraham)
"...Do not lay your hand on the lad, or do anything to him; for now I know that you fear God, since you have not withheld your son, your only son, from Me." Genesis 22:12

God says, "Take your rest from physical weariness and painful emotions. Release all this to Me. Do not seek to be fully understood by anyone but a loving God who holds all your tears in a bottle. I do know, My children, I do know. Is that enough for you?"

"O Lord, You have searched me and known me. You know my sitting down and my rising up; You understand my thought afar off. You comprehend my path and my lying down, and are acquainted with all my ways. For there is not a word on my tongue, but behold, O Lord, You know it altogether. You have hedged me behind and before, and laid Your hand upon me; such knowledge is too wonderful for me; it is high, I cannot attain it." Psalm 139:1-6

September 9

God says, "I want you to be replete with My Spirit, not deplete of My Spirit. I do not want you to be replete with flesh, but replete with Spirit. I want you to be deplete of flesh."

"Beloved, I beg you as sojourners and pilgrims, abstain from fleshly lusts which was against the soul." 1 Peter 2:11

God says, "Be not of this world. Be not of these people. Come apart and be ye separate, for I am making a new society of a remnant few who will be so peculiar they'll be mocked and laughed at. Are you mocked? Are you laughed at? Are you derided? Are you persecuted? For all that live just lives and godly lives in Christ Jesus shall suffer persecution. Are you so peculiar that people can tell you're a Christian without you saying so, and your demeanor so God-like that you put Him first in all you think and do and say?"

"But even if you should suffer for righteousness' sake, you are blessed. 'And do not be afraid of their threats, nor be troubled.'" 1 Peter 3:14

September 10

God says, "It is Gethsemane that brings the parting between those who are asleep and those who are alert as My Son was alert for those three hours."

> *"Then Christ said to them, 'My soul is exceedingly sorrowful, even to death. Stay here and watch with Me.' Then He came to the disciples and found them asleep, and said to Peter, 'What? Could you not watch with Me one hour?'...So He left them...and prayed the third time....Then He came to His disciples and said to them, 'Are you still sleeping and resting? Behold, the hour is at hand, and the Son of Man is being betrayed into the hands of sinners.'"* Matthew 26:38,40,44-45

God says, "The hour is late, and the nation is dark, and people are beginning to celebrate, even in the dark. But I say unto you that you who are the few, you who are those who will deny yourselves daily, take up your cross, and follow Me shall not ever regret doing that."

> *"I will set My tabernacle among you, and My soul shall not abhor you. I will walk among you and be your God, and you shall be My people."*
> Leviticus 26:11-12

September 11

God says, "The old nature is like a cloth thrown over the light of the word in the spirit of man. When it becomes a controlling influence in your life, it diffuses the light of the word so that My word is not free to perform the work to which it is sent to be executed."

"Then Jesus said to them, 'A little while longer the light is with you. Walk while you have the light, lest darkness overtake you; he who walks in darkness does not know where he is going. While you have the light, believe in the light, that you may become sons of light.'"
John 12:35-36a

God says, "It is the old nature that diffuses and suffocates the light in you. That is why Paul said, 'I am crucified with Christ, nevertheless, I live; but yet not I, not the light suffocator, and diffuser. It is Christ that lives or reflects Himself through me.'" (See Galatians 2:20.)

"For you died, and your life is hidden with Christ in God. When Christ who is our life appears, then you also will appear with Him in glory." Colossians 3:3-4

September 12

God says, "The enemy would lull you into apathy and a false sense of security, if he could. He is not apathetic. He is fully determined. Shore up your defenses. Awake to righteousness! The choice is yours. I could not be God, and decide for you."

> *"Blessed is the man who listens to me, watching daily at my gates, waiting at the posts of my doors. For whoever finds me, finds life, and obtains favor from the Lord."* Proverbs 8:34-35

God says, "It is a very serious thing to consider your spiritual growth in the many, many, many, many times and years you've been apathetic toward Me—you've never been hot for Me. My Son, Jesus Christ, says, 'Be hot or cold but don't be lukewarm.'"

> *"So then, because you are lukewarm, and neither cold nor hot, I will vomit you out of My mouth."* Revelation 3:16

September 13

God says, "It's a time to wake up from your sleep and your hibernation from Me. Do not pamper your flesh, My children. Do not let your mind have presence over My Spirit in you."

"...now it is high time to awake out of sleep; for now our salvation is nearer than when we first believed. The night is far spent, the day is at hand. Therefore let us cast off the works of darkness, and let us put on the armor of light."
Romans 13:11-12

God says, "I tell you to see the gravity of this hour, My people. It is not an hour to celebrate selfhood. It's an hour to celebrate the Christ of humanity, the Christ who has given you the way out. Take the escape from the men about you, for they will deceive you. They will lead you and lure you into a shallow indifference and apathy toward God."

"And we desire that each one of you show the same diligence to the full assurance of hope until the end, that you do not become sluggish, but imitate those who through faith and patience inherit the promises." Hebrews 6:11-12

September 14

God says, "Be thankful that God has made you for this hour; for this is an hour of greatness for some and an hour of apathy for others. Which camp will you be in? Will you waffle between two decisions? You must decide today in your heart that Christ is worth everything, more than the toys of this earth, more than all the joyful things the world presents to you which are pale beside the Lord God."

"Brethren, I do not count myself to have appre-hended; but one thing I do, forgetting those things which are behind and reaching forward to those things which are ahead, I press toward the goal for the prize of the upward call of God in Christ Jesus." Philippians 3:13-14

God says, "You must not linger any longer on the fence of procrastination, apathy, and spiritual contentment. Get within your heart, get within your spirit, and seek Me there, and so you can focus on My presence."

"I was in the Spirit on the Lord's Day, and I heard behind me a loud voice, as of a trumpet, saying, 'I am the Alpha and the Omega, the First and the Last...'" Revelation 1:10-11a

September 15

God says, "To ignore Me is fatal. To love Me is vital. Choose you this day whom you will serve, but as for My people and their people, they shall serve Me, the Lord." (See Joshua 24:15.)

"...I have set before you life and death, blessing and cursing; therefore choose life..."
Deuteronomy 30:19

God says, "You must think of the acts and decisions you're making today which are hardening you and compelling you to go with the world that is around you."

"Your word I have hidden in my heart, that I might not sin against You." Psalm 119:11

September 16

God says, "In the world you are in, everyone is daring to be as if they are God of their affairs. How many decisions do you make daily and weekly and monthly and yearly that were never confirmed by God? How many times have you decided for yourself, not God for yourself?"

"...So whatever I speak, I am saying [exactly] what My Father has told Me to say and in accordance with His instructions." John 12:50b (AMP)

God asks, "Do you decide for yourself rather than God for yourself?"

"For the others all seek [to advance] their own interests, not those of Jesus Christ (the Messiah)." Philippians 2:21 (AMP)

But what did Christ do?

"I can of Myself do nothing...because I do not seek My own will but the will of the Father who sent Me." John 5:30

September 17

Chiros moments occur in our lives when our future gets compressed in a moment of divine destiny. There is a divine call and a human choice involved. *Chiros* moments occur at an intersection in life, where we exist in an eternal moment. Some of these *chiros* moments can almost tear us apart as we wrestle with ourselves to choose God's way.

> *"...He touched the socket of his hip; and the socket...was out of joint as He wrestled with him. And He said, 'Your name shall no longer be called Jacob, but Israel; for you have struggled with God and with men, and have prevailed.'"* Genesis 32:25,28

It has been said there are two wills of God, but there is only one will of the Father, His perfect will. The other will that has been described is the permissive will—what God allows us to do by our own free choice. His perfect will is to have preeminence over our lives and for us to do His will. Christ Jesus is our example.

> *"Jesus said to them, 'My food is to do the will of Him who sent me, and to finish His work.'"* John 4:34

September 18

God says, "How many times, My sons, in your life have you said it was the right thing, and later I proved to you it was not the right thing? That's why I said let the words of your mouth, not My mouth, be few."

"Do not be rash with your mouth, and let not your heart utter anything hastily before God. For God is in heaven, and you on earth; therefore let your words be few." Ecclesiastes 5:2

God says, "You are all trying to anticipate that the unbelieving world will continue to produce what you believe you need for prosperity."

"And the world passes away and disappears, and with it...(the passionate desires, the lust) of it; but he who does the will of God and carries out His purposes in his life abides (remains) forever." 1 John 2:17 (AMP)

September 19

God says, "If you have confusion, do not blame it on Me, because you chose the way you've chosen. You will stumble and fall and be hurt often by the world, when you would not have had to, had you made the right decision at the right time."

"If you will listen diligently to the voice of the Lord your God, being watchful to do all His commandments which I command you this day, the Lord your God will set you high above all the nations of the earth." Deuteronomy 28:1 (AMP)

God says, "Ignore Me if you want. Keep Me away from your home, from your heart. Keep Me out of your daily affairs. That's your choice, for you have free will, but My will is still for you to do My will."

"So that he can no longer spend the rest of his natural life living by [his] human appetites and desires, but [he lives] for what God wills."
1 Peter 4:2 (AMP)

September 20

God says, "Be sensitive to Me. A man who is spirit operated is sensitive and obedient. Remember, I have said without holiness no man shall see God. Your living must be holy. If you say 'I do not want the flesh to go,' then you are saying you do not want the Spirit to come in all My glory. Flesh must be anathema to you. Flesh must be as the most severe poison to you. Abhor that which is evil and cleave to that which is good. Avoid the appearance of evil."

"Teach me to do Your will, for You are my God; let Your good Spirit lead me into a level country and into the land of uprightness."
Psalm 143:10 (AMP)

God says, "In academics you strive for excellence and perfection, but in the spiritual things you do not strive for excellence or for perfection. You are to be excellent and perfected. It is not a matter of striving, but it is a matter of being. You cannot sustain yourselves. Do not try. I sustain you, or you are not sustained. I sustain you as long as you are grafted into My total word."

"I will instruct you and teach you in the way you should go; I will guide you with My eye."
Psalm 32:8

September 21

God says, "Make up your mind today, because multitudes, multitudes are in the valley of decision. I shall make the choice for you, because it's already been made; and in your heart you know you are Mine today."

"To open their eyes and to turn them from darkness to light, and from the power of Satan to God, that they may receive forgiveness of sins and an inheritance among those who are sanctified by faith in Me." Acts 26:18

God says, "It's a late hour, and many of you are still tarrying by the idleness of your hands and the idleness of your heart, to seek Me with all your heart. What are you still waiting for? There comes a time when there is no more time. Your *chiros* moment [moment of choice] is passing."

"Only take heed to yourself, and diligently keep yourself, lest you forget the things your eyes have seen, and lest they depart from your heart all the days of your life..." Deuteronomy 4:9

September 22

God says, "The enemy and I are waiting for your choice to see if you will walk monistically [God-centered] in Me or dualistically [double-minded] in him."

"Multitudes, multitudes in the valley of decision! For the day of the Lord is near in the valley of decision." Joel 3:14

The growth of the enemy is much like moss growing on rocks. It can choke out the truth.

God needs to see us as being active for the Lord.

God says, "Either I am your Lord, or I am not. Declare it so. No declaration is a declaration. No decision is a decision. No choice is a choice."

September 23

God says, "What is conceived in the mind is carried out in the body. Thus, one's whole tripartite being must be presented by a decisive act of the will to God."

Yielding must not be thought of simply as a willingness to do a certain thing. Rather, it consists of dedication and surrender by a person to do whatever God asks.

"Therefore, beloved, looking forward to these things, be diligent to be found by Him in peace, without spot and blameless." 2 Peter 3:14

God says, "Choice comes when you can choose to change your imperfections for God's perfections."

"But you are a chosen race, a royal priesthood, a dedicated nation, [God's] own purchased, special people, that you may set forth the wonderful deeds and display the virtues and perfections of Him who called you out of darkness into His marvelous light." 1 Peter 2:9 (AMP)

September 24

God asks, "Do you want to come into the light of His presence or remain on the threshold or outside, content to be who you are, but not who My Christ is?"

"Behold, I stand at the door and knock; if anyone hears and listens to and heeds My voice and opens the door, I will come in to him..."
Revelation 3:20 (AMP)

God says, "I do long for you to come to a place where you can say freely, 'It doesn't matter what the consequences are. If it's not of God, let the consequences fall wherever they may be, whatever they may be. As for me and my house, we shall serve the Lord.'"

"Let us hold fast the confession of our hope without wavering, for He who promised is faithful." Hebrews 10:23

"Now faith is the substance of things hoped for, the evidence of things not seen." Hebrews 11:1

September 25

$God\ says,$ "What opportunities you have now are no less nor greater than you have ever had with Me. Whatever the plan that was presented to you, I am God; I change not."

"For I am the Lord, I do not change…"
Malachi 3:6a

"Jesus Christ is the same yesterday, today, and forever." Hebrews 13:8

"Therefore, brethren, be even more diligent to make your calling and election sure, for if you do these things you will never stumble."
2 Peter 1:10

$God\ says,$ "It's time to withdraw yourselves from the world, and that is a very radical thought. But I've said, have I not, that those who are friends of the world cannot be My friend, but I said they are My enemy. Those who have put the friendship of the world before My friendship, before My relationship with them, are enemies of God. Anyone who builds you up and does not build Me up is one who is seeking the favor of men."

"You are My friends if you keep on doing the things which I command you to do."
John 15:14 (AMP)

September 26

God says, "There is no guilt in God's kingdom. God does not find guilt. There is need of God's love and correction, because without His correction, there can be no *agape* love. Don't take guilt on yourself. Take Christ on yourself."

> *"Therefore, having been justified by faith, we have peace with God through our Lord Jesus Christ, through whom also we have access by faith into this grace in which we stand, and rejoice in hope of the glory of God."* Romans 5:1-2

God says, "I will lead, and you will follow, and you will not lead Me. I will lead you, though you think you're leading. Those may be the times of greatest weakness within you, because you have more propensity to fall to the wiles of the evil one."

> *"... a bondservant of Christ, greets you, always laboring fervently for you in prayers, that you may stand perfect and complete in all the will of God."* Colossians 4:12

> *"Then the word of the Lord came to me, saying: 'O house of Israel, can I not do with you as this potter?' says the Lord. 'Look, as the clay is in the potter's hand, so are you in My hand, O house of Israel!'"* Jeremiah 18:6

September 27

Have you learned to shield yourself from the conviction God brings to you through His word and Spirit?

"But we have renounced the hidden things of shame, not walking in craftiness nor handling the word of God deceitfully..." 2 Corinthians 4:2a

"I acknowledged my sin to You, and my iniquity I have not hidden..." Psalm 32:5a

God says, "I will change those who will change. I will make the impossible possible. I will make sure My Holy Spirit will be right there convicting; but you must have a willingness and a desire for change."

"Thus says the Lord, your Redeemer, the Holy One of Israel: I am the Lord your God, Who teaches you to profit, Who leads you by the way you should go." Isaiah 48:17

September 28

God says, "You must not put restrictions on what I can do or what you can do. You must know that you can do all things through Christ who strengthens you."

> *"Behold, I am the Lord, the God of all flesh. Is there anything too hard for Me?"* Jeremiah 32:27

While you say, "How can it be done?", God says, "Why is it not done?"

> *"Fear not, for I am with you; Be not dismayed, for I am your God. I will strengthen you, yes, I will help you, I will uphold you with My right-eous right hand."* Isaiah 41:10

September 29

God says, "A questioning spirit does not have peace. It ties with uncertainty, doubt, and confusion."

"Commit your works to the Lord, and your thoughts will be established." Proverbs 16:3

God says, "You see, I have more love for those who accept without question than those who question in order to accept Me."

(But Thomas said) "... 'Unless I see in His hands the print of the nails, and put my finger into the print of the nails, and my hand into His side, I will not believe.' Jesus said to him, 'Thomas, because you have seen Me, you have believed. Blessed are those who have not seen and yet have believed.'" John 20:25b, 29

Thomas put conditions on his believing. How often do we put conditions on our believing?

September 30

God says, "Compromise is double-mindedness. You have two minds. Many people compromise because they can't find peace, but compromise causes you to be indecisive and faithless."

"But let him ask in faith, with no doubting, for he who doubts is like a wave of the sea driven and tossed by the wind." James 1:6

Satan causes us to become an enemy of ourselves by causing us to compromise the truth in our lives. He asks, "Has God really said...," and if we listen, the seed of compromise has been planted.

"Then the man said, 'The woman whom You gave to be with me, she gave me of the tree, and I ate.' And the Lord God said to the woman, 'What is this you have done?' And the woman said, 'The serpent deceived me, and I ate.'"
Genesis 3:12-13

October 1

Compromise is abandoning your stand in Jesus Christ. Compromise is saying no to God. Compromise leads you into doorways of captivity.

Are you being seduced into compromise? Be alert! Compromise will turn your heart away from God.

> *"For we can do nothing against the truth, but for the truth."* 2 Corinthians 13:8

God says, "You have a right to say no to sin. You have a right to say yes to good. You have a right to say no to the wrong choice."

Don't say yes to what God says no to. Say yes to what God would say yes to, if He were living in you, and He does!

> *"Now he who keeps His commandments abides in Him, and He in him. And by this we know that He abides in us, by the Spirit whom He has given us."* 1 John 3:24

October 2

Do not compromise. Compromise is saying no to God. Surrender means saying yes.

Compromise leads to more compromise and more compromise until you are living a life of compromise.

> *"Bring forth fruit that is consistent with repentance [let your lives prove your change of heart]."* Matthew 3:8 (AMP)

God says, "When you don't know you're under God's rule, your conscience will be less strict. When you do those things that are compromise, you'll find them comfortable to do."

God doesn't divorce Himself from us. In compromise, we have done the divorcing.

> *"There is a way that seems right to a man, but its end is the way of death."* Proverbs 16:25

> *"He who covers his sins will not prosper, but whoever confesses and forsakes them will have mercy."* Proverbs 28:13

October 3

God asks, "Why do we not have enough reverence and awe of the Lord to stand uncompromising for Him?"

Compromise brings in condemnation.

"Therefore, [there is] now no condemnation (no adjudging guilty of wrong) for those who are in Christ Jesus, who live [and] walk not after the dictates of the flesh, but after the dictates of the Spirit." Romans 8:1 (AMP)

"...the [uncompromisingly] righteous have an everlasting foundation." Proverbs 10:25b (AMP)

God says, "You haven't gone this far to halt between two opinions. The two opinions are: you can either give in and yield and compromise, or you can say no to anything the enemy offers."

"Elijah came near to all the people and said, 'How long will you halt and limp between two opinions? If the Lord is God, follow Him! But if Baal, then follow him.' And the people did not answer him a word." 1 Kings 18:21 (AMP)

October 4

God asks, "What is holiness but the presence of the Lord in your life in every decision, thought, and deed?"

"Your people shall be volunteers in the day of Your power; in the beauties of holiness, from the womb of the morning, You have the dew of Your youth." Psalm 110:3

God says, "Notice over and over the Spirit is referred to as 'holy.' Holy by men's standards is not holy with Me—it is unholy."

"But we are all like an unclean thing, and our righteousnesses are like filthy rags..." Isaiah 64:6a

If as a believer, you are filled with the Holy Spirit, your conduct and character should reflect His holiness. The Holy Spirit gives you a desire to be holy.

October 5

God asks, "Has My standard of holiness brought about a reaction of submission and obedience to My cleansing power in the written and living word in you? If it is not so, then you have not arrived, and you have far to go."

"If you endure chastening, God deals with you as with sons...but if you are without chastening...then you are illegitimate and not sons. Furthermore, we have had human fathers who corrected us, and we paid them respect. Shall we not much more readily be in subjection to the Father of spirits and live? For they indeed for a few days chastened us as seemed best to them, but He for our profit, that we may be partakers of His holiness." Hebrews 12:7-10

God says, "You cannot demand purity and holiness of your children until it is in you. You cannot lift up a standard before your children of your flesh until you are an example before Me of children of My faith and spiritual nature."

"But as He who called you is holy, you also be holy in all your conduct, because it is written, 'Be holy, for I am holy.'" 1 Peter 1:15-16

October 6

God says, "Spiritual fasting is that daily meditative fasting from the physical plane and from the thoughts of the natural, carnal man."

"Let no one deceive himself. If anyone among you seems to be wise in this age, let him become a fool that he may become wise. For the wisdom of this world is foolishness with God. For it is written, 'He catches the wise in their own craftiness.'" 1 Corinthians 3:18-19

God says, "Spend time in a spiritual fast to relieve yourself of all those things that are detrimental to your health. Fast because you are lovesick for the Bridegroom."

"And Jesus said to them, 'Can the friends of the Bridegroom mourn as long as the Bridegroom is with them? But the days will come when the Bridegroom will be taken away from them, and then they will fast.'" Matthew 9:15

"Is this not the fast that I have chosen: to loose the bonds of wickedness, to undo the heavy burdens, to let the oppressed go free, and that you break every yoke?" Isaiah 58:6

October 7

God says, "I cannot lead you if you cannot hear Me, so if you're not hearing My voice, you should stop and sit down, and you should go to Me and stay in My presence until you hear My voice."

> *"...He wakens me morning by morning, He wakens my ear to hear as a disciple [as one who is taught]. The Lord has opened my ear..."*
> Isaiah 50:4b-5a (AMP)

As lovers of Christ, we are to be living the Christ-life which must include the Shepherd's voice.

God says His voice must be the most important voice we hear. We are to know it intimately and seek to follow His voice fully.

The Chief Shepherd and Bishop of our souls says,

> *"The sheep that are My own hear and are listening to My voice; and I know them, and they follow Me."* John 10:27 (AMP)

October 8

God says, "And you must learn to hear from Me. If you cannot hear for yourselves, listen to someone who hears."

"...Everyone who is of the truth hears My voice." John 18:37b

"...Be careful what you are hearing. The measure [of thought and study] you give [to the truth you hear] will be the measure... that comes back to you—and more [besides] will be given to you who hear." Mark 4:24 (AMP)

God says, "Listen for My voice. Listen for My voice. Hear Me and live. Tell the world to hear Me. Tell them to listen to My voice while there is time, while there is time. Listen to My voice and live."

"Most assuredly, I say to you, the hour is coming, and now is, when the dead will hear the voice of the Son of God; and those who hear will live." John 5:25

"Incline your ear, and come to Me. Hear, and your soul shall live..." Isaiah 55:3a

October 9

God says, "You must seek Me and listen to Me. The sound of My voice must be as real to you, as important to hear as anything in the world. Yes, more important than any voice you hear now. My voice must be the highest priority. Take time to sit before Me."

"... and He calls His own sheep by name and leads them out. And when He brings out His own sheep, He goes before them; and the sheep follow Him, for they know His voice. ...they do not know the voice of strangers." John 10:3b-4,5b

God asks, "How can My Spirit show you the truth, and teach you the truth, and show you things to come, except the voice of God be heard among you?"

"However, when He, the Spirit of truth, has come, He will guide you into all truth; for He will not speak on His own authority, but whatever He hears He will speak; and He will tell you things to come. He will glorify Me, for He will take of what is Mine and declare it to you." John 16:13-14

We must have ears to hear what the Spirit declares to us.

October 10

God says, "You need the words I give you, for the words are wholesome. The words are good. Seek them, and *selah* them, because they shall cause you to live; and they shall cause your natural man to begin to change and to detest the world."

> *"My son, give attention to my words; incline your ear to my sayings. Do not let them depart from your eyes; keep them in the midst of your heart; for they are life to those who find them, and health to all their flesh."* Proverbs 4:20-22

God says, "True compassion is learning to say no when I say no and to say yes when I say yes."

> *"Then Jesus, looking at him, loved him, and said to him, 'One thing you lack: Go your way, sell whatever you have and give to the poor, and you will have treasure in heaven; and come, take up the cross, and follow Me.' But he was sad at this word, and went away sorrowful, for he had great possessions."* Mark 10:21-22

October 11

God says, "When your spirit walks by the voice of God, then your flesh will follow, because flesh is weak, and that is an advantage. The Spirit takes precedence over the flesh."

"Your ears shall hear a word behind you, saying, 'This is the way, walk in it', whenever you turn to the right hand or whenever you turn to the left." Isaiah 30:21

God says, "I, the Father, am Abba to those who seek Him, to those who hear His voice, to those who commune with Him, to those who trust Him."

"And because you are sons, God has sent forth the Spirit of His Son into your hearts, crying out, 'Abba, Father!' Therefore you are no longer a slave but a son, and if a son, then an heir of God through Christ." Galatians 4:6

October 12

God says, "There are many words you're hearing today. Which words are you drawn to? Which words are you preferring? The words of men or the words of God? For where your heart is there is your treasure."

"...Let your heart retain my words; Keep my commands, and live. Get wisdom! Get understanding! Do not forget, nor turn away from the words of my mouth." Proverbs 4:4-5

God says, "Just listen to the small voice inside you. When you know it's not you, open your mouth. I'll fill it. When you have that tugging knowledge inside that God's wanting you to speak, just open your mouth by faith. I shall provide the words, for if you provide the words by your mind, it's carnal; but do this by faith today. Let My voice speak within you."

"But when they deliver you up, do not worry about how or what you should speak. For it will be given to you in that hour what you should speak; for it is not you who speak, but the Spirit of your Father who speaks in you."
Matthew 10:19-20

October 13

God says, "The vocabulary I want among you is 'God says, God says, God says, God says.' I want all the body of Christ to be able to hear the voice of the Shepherd, because My sheep all hear My voice and follow Me. They have one agreement—that the word is what keeps them cohesive, as individual members, into one corporate body."

" '...My Spirit who is upon you, and My words which I have put in your mouth, shall not depart from your mouth, nor from the mouth of your descendants, nor from the mouth of your descendants' descendants,' says the Lord, 'from this time and forevermore.'" Isaiah 59:21

God says, "That's the difference between your world and My realm. In My realm everyone wants thus saith the Lord and wants the voice of the Father, even My Son, who intercedes for you now. He wants to be submissive to anything I say. He doesn't even want to think His own thoughts."

"And He who sent Me is with Me. The Father has not left Me alone, for I always do those things that please Him." John 8:29

October 14

God says, "It will be My word that will stand when heaven and earth pass away, for My word will stand forever. When you find a vessel who speaks that word, you've found Me. When you see one who is an oracle, who delivers the word without any hesitation in the Spirit, and not by his mind's effort or by his own understanding, you then know you are living by every word that comes out of My mouth, should you hear, and should you obey the word that comes."

*"For prophecy never came by the will of man,
but holy men of God spoke as they were moved
by the Holy Spirit."* 2 Peter 1:21

God says, "I said if any man speaks, let him speak as the spokesman of God. If any man speaks as God's man, he must speak as the oracle of God, as one who reflects and hears within him the word of God, and speaks it forth. (See 1 Peter 4:11.) Speak it forth, not from your understanding. Speak it forth from your heart, and it shall be truly My *rhema*."

October 15

You say, "Lord, I expect the best from You. I do expect You to give me only Your best. And if my best that I desire is not as good as Yours, I surrender it to You, and ask You to give me only Your best in every situation I'm in.

Expect every day to be a new day for you, and a new day for you in Him.

God says, "Do not be limited by anything that is limiting—your mind, your reason, your wisdom, your ability. I, the Lord, am the only One that is unlimited, and I will not limit you. You are unlimited in what you can expect from Me."

"Jesus said to him, 'If you can believe, all things are possible to him who believes.'" Mark 9:23

October 16

God says, "This is the day of good things."

How would our day go if we began each morning with this confession, "This is the day of good things"? God says He's made the sun to shine and He's given us a place in the family of God and eternal life without qualifications. We did not earn it, but God gave it freely. These things alone should cause us to say, "This is the day of good things."

We are convinced that God is Who He says He is, that He is able to do all things, and with God, all things are possible, that nothing is impossible.

"The Lord of hosts has sworn, saying, 'Surely, as I have thought, so it shall come to pass, and as I have purposed, so it shall stand...' for the Lord of hosts has purposed, and who will annul it? His hand is stretched out, and who will turn it back?" Isaiah 14:24,27

October 17

God says, "You must be willing to let everything be broken that has been put on the altar of expediency. Let everything be broken. Expect nothing of this world's gain. Expect only the riches of Christ. Expect it and prepare to be recipients of it."

"He who trusts in his riches will fall, but the righteous will flourish like foliage." Proverbs 11:28

"The eyes of your understanding being enlightened; that you may know what is the hope of His calling, what are the riches of the glory of His inheritance in the saints." Ephesians 1:18

Wait on the Lord in you and expect to wait until He appears.

"For God alone my soul waits in silence; from Him comes my salvation." Psalm 62:1 (AMP)

"Wait and hope for and expect the Lord; be brave and of good courage and let your heart be stout and enduring. Yes, wait for and hope for and expect the Lord." Psalm 27:14 (AMP)

October 18

God says, "When you forgive, it takes a lot of pain away when you realize you've let that hurt go. You no longer hold aught against anyone. You must be able to forgive to get the peace that passes all understanding."

"Therefore, as the elect of God, holy and beloved, put on tender mercies, kindness, humility, meekness, longsuffering; bearing with one another, and forgiving one another, if anyone has a complaint against another; even as Christ forgave you, so you also must do. But above all these things put on love, which is the bond of perfection." Colossians 3:12-14

God says, "One of the characteristics of the attribute of a growing son of God is that he loves more. He forgives easily and quickly. He doesn't care who the source of the hatred is. He forgives anyway, as Christ does. Christ forgives all flesh if they repent."

An immortal soul and spirit is beyond all price.

"And be kind to one another, tenderhearted, forgiving one another, even as God in Christ forgave you." Ephesians 4:32

October 19

Grace is getting something you don't deserve.

Mercy is not getting something you do deserve.

"For by grace you have been saved through faith, and that not of yourselves; it is the gift of God." Ephesians 2:8

"Through the Lord's mercies we are not consumed, because His compassions fail not." Lamentations 3:22

God says, "For your God is a God of strength. He is a God of solace. He's compassionate. He's forgiving. He's loving. He is one who can erase from even your mind the evil of the past, because the past is not existent when a Christian realizes that he's forgiven before and not afterwards."

"For You, Lord, are good, and ready to forgive, and abundant in mercy to all those who call upon You." Psalm 86:5

"...Forgive, and you will be forgiven." Luke 6:37c

October 20

God says, "Rise up. That's where I am. Don't fall. That's where I am not. My men are men who stand and walk and climb and run—who don't know what opposition is before the power of the Holy Spirit."

"But those who wait on the Lord shall renew their strength; they shall mount up with wings like eagles, they shall run and not be weary, and they shall walk and not faint." Isaiah 40:31

God says, "My Son urges you this day from His throne as He intercedes for you, to come, arise in the Spirit, and ascend with Him as He ascended, to come boldly in spirit and truth before My throne, that you may receive mercy and grace."

"Let us therefore come boldly to the throne of grace, that we may obtain mercy and find grace to help in time of need." Hebrews 4:16

"God is Spirit, and those who worship Him must worship in spirit and truth." John 4:24

October 21

God says, "Come up, come out, and learn of Me."

We are to come up in the Spirit and out of ourselves and be separated so that we are free to learn of God.

> *"But you, beloved, build yourselves up [founded]*
> *on your most holy faith [make progress, rise like*
> *an edifice higher and higher], praying in the*
> *Holy Spirit; guard and keep yourselves in the*
> *love of God..."* Jude 20-21a (AMP)

God says, "Rising up means a total withdrawal from all things carnal, all things corruptive, all things disruptive, all things of the flesh. It means denying yourself any access to things in the physical realm, so that you can keep your eyes and your ears fully attuned to see, hear, and taste the things of God in the spiritual realm."

> *"...when you received the word of God which*
> *you heard from us, you welcomed it not as the*
> *word of men, but as it is in truth, the word of*
> *God, which also effectively works in you who*
> *believe."* 1 Thessalonians 2:13

October 22

God asks, "Are you weary of this world? Then come up and ascend in Me. Ascend in Me and find out the truth that My love is far more enjoyable than all the thrills and chills and all the things you try to enjoy in this earth. They're anathema to Me, and they will finally be anathema to you if you mature."

> *"Truly my soul silently waits for God! From Him comes my salvation. He only is my rock and my salvation. He is my defense; I shall not be greatly moved. My soul, wait silently for God alone, for my expectation is from Him. Trust in Him at all times, you people; Pour out your heart before Him: God is a refuge for us."*
>
> Psalm 62:1-2,5,8

God says, "Let there be a rest from the weary things. The weary things are the lesser things. They are the things that weary you. Let there be a rest from them. They are the things that hassle and trouble, that undermine and delude, frustrate and hurt you. Rise up, O men of God. Have done with lesser things. Prepare your heart, mind, soul, and strength to serve the King of kings."

October 23

A walk with Christ will mean death to your stubbornness but life to your willingness.

There cannot be obedience to Christ without a word from God. Obedience means to hear something and then submit to it.

"Therefore let that abide in you which you heard from the beginning. If what you heard from the beginning abides in you, you also will abide in the Son and the Father." 1 John 2:24

"The Lord God has opened My ear; and I was not rebellious, nor did I turn away." Isaiah 50:5

God says, "I am alive forevermore, and none shall stand against My voice, for it shall prevail. Your solace and your secret place to come to Me is within your spirit where I dwell in the Holy of Holies in those who have opened their hearts to Me. I know those who are Mine. The sheep of My fold shall never stray; for they have heard the voice of God, and they will follow no other allegiance."

October 24

Jesus Christ is the fulfiller of every man's true self.

> *"And now, little children, abide in Him, that when He appears, we may have confidence and not be ashamed at His coming."* 1 John 2:28

Settle the war in yourself with the word of God.

Jesus Christ is a love chamber! He is a companion for life and for eternity.

> *"Let us be glad and rejoice and give Him glory, for the marriage of the Lamb has come, and His wife has made herself ready."* Revelation 19:7

> *"And I heard a loud voice from heaven saying, 'Behold, the tabernacle of God is with men, and He will dwell with them, and they shall be His people. God Himself will be with them and be their God.'"* Revelation 21:3

October 25

God says, "If your spirit is not tuned on My frequency, then you will only receive the echo of what I transmit. It's carried along the corridors of the spiritual highway between you and Me. It is not a matter of My condescending to come down on your level to speak to you that you might see and hear; it is a matter of you coming up hither. If My laws are perfect, then you must receive them perfectly. You must become acclimatized to My environment, not Me to yours."

"Lead me in Your truth and teach me, for You are the God of my salvation; on You I wait all the day." Psalm 25:5

God says, "I will speak to you as little ones who need to cut the cord of your intellect which binds you to the word of man. Open the door of your hearts that you might receive the true, pure, uncontradictable word of God. You who meditate in spirit and in truth will learn of Me. You who do not will learn of another, for another has come to rule this earth."

October 26

If we are Christians, we are the spiritual universe of God.

"You also, as living stones, are being built up a spiritual house, a holy priesthood, to offer up spiritual sacrifices acceptable to God through Jesus Christ." 1 Peter 2:5

God is saying to you, you don't have to be broken, but you may be broken because God wants you to come to an end of yourself and reach the beginning of your life in Christ in genuine spirit and truth.

"And I am convinced and sure of this very thing, that He Who began a good work in you will continue until the day of Jesus Christ...developing [that good work] and perfecting and bringing it to full completion in you." Philippians 1:6 (AMP)

October 27

God says, "You must not look unto yourself and introspectively focus on your problem. You must focus on the answer, and the answer is Christ within you, your hope of glory."

> *"To them God willed to make known what are the riches of the glory...which is Christ in you, the hope of glory."* Colossians 1:27

Nothing compares to the promise I have in You, Lord.

> *"So that the man of God may be complete,... well-fitted and thoroughly equipped for every good work."* 2 Timothy 3:17 (AMP)

God says, "If you want to be like My Son Jesus, then you must be on your way to laying down your self, your pride, your reasoning, and your ability to logically figure out this problem or that."

October 28

Jesus Christ, Lord of lords and King of kings, can do anything, and yet He still felt the need to pray fervently to the Father.

The Son of God also feared. He had a reverential fear of His Father.

"Who, in the days of His flesh, when He had offered up prayers and supplications, with vehement cries and tears to Him who was able to save Him from death, and was heard because of His godly fear, though He was a Son, yet He learned obedience by the things which He suffered." Hebrews 5:7-8

God says, "I sent My Son to be flesh for you, that through flesh you might see the veil can be rent through your heart; and when the heart is right before Me, then I can make His life your life, for I seek to replace your life with His life."

"And Jesus cried out again with a loud voice, and yielded up His spirit. Then, behold, the veil of the temple was torn in two from top to bottom..." Matthew 27:50-51

"This hope we have as an anchor of the soul, both sure and steadfast, and which enters the Presence behind the veil." Hebrews 6:19

October 29

God says, "Do not dismiss Me from your heart, because you're part of the world's fray and warfare. Do not stray from Me today, because you do not know the way outside of My Son. My Son is the only One to point to the way, the truth, and the life, and He is the way, the truth, and the life."

"Jesus said to him, I am the way, the truth, and the life. No one comes to the Father except through Me." John 14:6

Christ says, "I am seated in your heart."

Do we treat Him as the honored guest?

"My heart also instructs me in the right seasons. I have set the Lord always before me."
Psalms 16:7b-8a

October 30

God says, "I, your Jesus, but now the risen Christ, reach out My arms of love and forgiveness, saying, 'Accept My gifts. They are without cost.' Christ is walking throughout the hearts of men who are turned toward Him this day."

> *"Jesus answered and said to her, 'If you knew*
> *the gift of God, and who it is who says to you,*
> *"Give Me a drink," you would have asked Him,*
> *and He would have given you living water.'"*
> John 4:10

God says, "You received My word of salvation, now receive My word of life and let your spirit grow. Let your faith grow through My word, and practice My word daily. Don't just confess it. Live by it. Put it into action. Believe it. Convince yourself that it is truth and the only true thing you have."

> *"...Do not be faithless and incredulous, but [stop*
> *your unbelief and] believe!...Blessed and happy*
> *and to be envied are those who have never seen*
> *Me and yet have believed..."* John 20:27b,29b (AMP)

October 31

God says, "The joy of My salvation is something you will never forget, for I will walk with you in sorrows. I will walk with you in darkness. When you reach out your hand, I'll touch you. When you fall in My arms, I will shield you today. Oh, come into My kingdom and pray."

"And the grace of our Lord was exceedingly abundant, with faith and love which are in Christ Jesus." 1 Timothy 1:14

In God we have all the possibilities of becoming a different creature than we are.

"Therefore if any person is [ingrafted] in Christ (the Messiah) he is a new creation (he is a new creature altogether); the old [previous moral and spiritual condition] has passed away. Behold, the fresh and new has come!"
2 Corinthians 5:17 (AMP)

November 1

God says about Himself, "If God were not love, the foundation of the whole universe would collapse. One of His greatest blessings is His unconditional love for you, though no one else love you in the world. He will love you and be with you in eternity, if you take His hand."

God says, "Take My hand today through My Son, and reach out for joy and peace and righteousness throughout all time to come, an endless eternity."

When we turn our heart to the Lord, opening ourselves to Him:

> *"He dawns on them like the morning light when the sun rises on a cloudless morning, when the tender grass springs out of the earth through clear shining after rain."* 2 Samuel 23:4 (AMP)

November 2

God says, "I am the God that is of newness. Everything I do is a new thing in you."

"And have clothed yourselves with the new [spiritual self], which is [ever in the process of being] renewed..." Colossians 3:10 (AMP)

God says, "I am wanting to complete that which concerns you. I do not want to wait. Why do you want to wait? Let all go and let Me come in."

"...Behold, now is the accepted time; behold, now is the day of salvation." 2 Corinthians 6:2b

November 3

God says, "While you may have already gone through a spiritual experience of being rebirthed from above, you need to be rebirthed in the image of My Son."

> *"And all of us, as with unveiled face, [because we] continued to behold [in the Word of God] as in a mirror the glory of the Lord, are constantly being transfigured into His very own image in ever increasing splendor and from one degree of glory to another; [for this comes] from the Lord [Who is] the Spirit."* 2 Corinthians 3:18 (AMP)

When you first received salvation, it was for yourself to deliver you from sin. You should now ask God to save you for His purposes and not your own.

> *"...But now, once at the end of the ages, He has appeared to put away sin by the sacrifice of Himself. So Christ was offered once to bear the sins of many. To those who eagerly wait for Him He will appear a second time, apart from sin, for salvation."* Hebrews 9:26b,28

November 4

God says, "For the former things have passed away, and the old things are gone. And the tracks you made in the sand of life are long swept away, and no one can follow the trail of your sinful past."

"Do not remember the former things, nor consider the things of old. Behold, I will do a new thing, Now it shall spring forth; shall you not know it..." Isaiah 43:18-19

God says, "It seems hard, but I love you, and I understand, and I give you grace. Where sin abounds, grace much more abounds. We're over here in the world where there's no controversy, no division, no confusion, no trouble, no anxiety, no care. We want you to have the same benefits of your salvation."

"Blessed be the Lord, who daily loads us with benefits, the God of our salvation! Selah"
Psalm 68:19

"What shall I render to the Lord for all His benefits toward me? [How can I repay Him for all His bountiful blessings?]" Psalm 116:12 (AMP)

November 5

God says, "You must honor Me with your heart and then with your lips; for how are you saved? You are saved by believing in your heart and confessing with your mouth; not by confessing with your mouth and then believing in your heart. For confession with the mouth without the heart belief is fruitless."

"But what does it say? 'The word is near you, even in your mouth and in your heart'...For with the heart one believes unto righteousness, and with the mouth confession is made unto salvation." Romans 10:8,10

God says, "My praise begins in the public arena. To prove that you are Mine, you must say so, say so—not just when you are cloistered inside, but when you are cloistered in the world where no one says so. No one says so. Do not fall silent because others fall silent. Lift up your voices on high and let people know you are a peculiar people, sold out to the God who died for every man that they might live."

"Go, stand in the temple and speak to the people all the words of life." Acts 5:20

November 6

God says, "I made all you see and all that you cannot see. I am Lord of infinity, and of creation, and of your universe. I've made My kingdom a realm of spirit men who love Me, awaiting with anticipation the return of My Son, and crying out, 'Maranatha, come quickly, Lord Jesus.'"

"And now, Israel, what does the Lord your God require of you, but to fear the Lord your God, to walk in all His ways and to love Him, to serve the Lord your God with all your heart and with all your soul." Deuteronomy 10:12

God says, "My word is not gray. It's not black, it's white. It's light, it's truth. It's the truthseeker's path to safety, and you must speak to your mind and bring it under subjection. Cast down all imaginations and all vain thoughts that do not bring peace but bring disorder and confusion. You must say, 'Be gone, be gone, oh natural thought; for I will not lean on the arm of flesh, and I will not listen to my own understanding.'"

"(Yes, a sword will pierce through your own soul also), that the thoughts of many hearts may be revealed." Luke 2:35

November 7

God says, "By your fruit you shall be known."

"When you bear (produce) much fruit, My Father is honored and glorified, and you show and prove yourselves to be true followers of Mine." John 15:8 (AMP)

"Therefore, you will fully know them by their fruits." Matthew 7:20 (AMP)

God says, "Be an example to others of who you are by the fruit you bear, by the words you hear, by what you live by, walk by, think by, talk about. Let every conversation be chaste and without any blemish."

"...but be an example to the believers in word, in conduct, in love, in spirit, in faith, in purity."
1 Timothy 4:12

November 8

God says, "If only the world could see in you Me, and not you, it would be very, very pleasing to Me. That's when each of you are indistinguishable to others, as far as individuality is concerned."

The greatest gift we can give God is the character of Christ formed in us.

> *"There is one body and one Spirit, just as you were called in one hope of your calling; one Lord, one faith, one baptism; one God and Father of all, who is above all, and through all, and in you all."* Ephesians 4:4-6

God says, "You must find a way to bond to Me until I cannot be separated from what you do, say, and think; and where you walk and what you say and what you do."

We say, "So come, Holy Spirit, and hold each of us tight in the arms of Your comforting truth."

> *"So that they should seek the Lord, in the hope they might grope for Him and find Him, though He is not far from each one of us; for in Him we live and move and have our being..."* Acts 17:27-28a

November 9

God says, "Make every aspect of your lives be without question. Do not ever mediate the truth and do not ever be dishonest in your ways."

"He who works deceit shall not dwell within my house; he who tells lies shall not continue in my presence." Psalm 101:7

"Buy the truth, and do not sell it. Also wisdom and instruction and understanding."
Proverbs 23:23

God says, "Your future depends on your walk. You will either walk uprightly with My approval and My word, and walk by My Spirit; or you will walk crippled, and you will be defeated."

"For the Lord God is a sun and shield; the Lord will give grace and glory; no good thing will He withhold from those who walk uprightly. O Lord of hosts, blessed is the man who trusts in You!" Psalm 84:11-12

November 10

The ultimate reward for reading and meditating in the Scriptures is that you will fall deeply in love with the author, God Himself.

> *"My soul waits for the Lord more than those
> who watch for the morning—yes, more than
> those who watch for the morning."* Psalm 130:6

God says, "Subdue the kingdoms of the mind. There is where the enemy wages war against My beloved church. Awake to righteousness."

> *"Do not withhold Your tender mercies from me,
> O Lord; let Your lovingkindness and Your truth
> continually preserve me."* Psalm 40:11

November 11

God says, "Be faithful in those things I have called you to. I will make you faithful over much. But I want those who are willing, and willing to be used by Me, willing to not count the cost, willing to go beyond the point of no return with Me, willing to be used even when your body is weary, and when you are tired, willing to say yes to Me."

"Then he [Nehemiah] read from it...from morning until midday, before the men and women and those who could understand; and the ears of all the people were attentive to the Book of the Law." Nehemiah 8:3

Our spiritual education begins when we seek God.

"But seek first the kingdom of God and His righteousness, and all these things shall be added to you." Matthew 6:33

"Talk no more so very proudly; let no arrogance come from your mouth, for the Lord is the God of knowledge; and by Him actions are weighed." 1 Samuel 2:3

November 12

God says, "What can I do with two or more who will agree to My will, and implement it? God and one are a majority, if the one is being led by My Holy Spirit. Remember, you have your cross of daily denial you must take up in order to follow Me. You must realize until Christ is fully formed within you, you are still groping in half light, trying to find your Lord."

"I have restrained my feet from every evil way, that I may keep Your word." Psalm 119:101

"I will [not merely walk, but] run the way of Your commandments, when You give me a heart that is willing." Psalm 119:32 (AMP)

God says, "Unless you hear My voice, you cannot know. Unless you comprehend, you cannot apprehend."

"That I may make you know the certainty of the words of truth, that you may answer words of truth to those who send to you." Proverbs 22:21

November 13

God says, "My nature is the word I have spoken. My word is My nature. My nature is My word, and it's a river. It's a river of cleansing. It's a river of life. It's a river of revelation. It's a river of safety. It's a river of comfort. It's a river of hope. It's a river of refreshing. It's a river of renewal. This river flows from My Spirit into yours. It's a river of everlasting waters."

"Sanctify them [purify, consecrate, separate them for Yourself, make them holy] by truth; Your word is truth." John 17:17 (AMP)

God says, "You walk on the water of My word, for the river shall not hurt you. The river shall change your nature. Let My word dwell in you richly in all wisdom. Teach and admonish one another."

"Rather, let our lives lovingly express truth [in all things, speaking truly, dealing truly, living truly]. Enfolded in love, let us grow up in every way and in all things into Him who is the Head, [even] Christ (the Messiah, the Anointed One)." Ephesians 4:15 (AMP)

November 14

God says, "Do not miss any of My word, because it's like picking and choosing—you can not do that. You are to take all of My word, because you must taste and see that the Lord is good. Come to Me through the word that's softened your heart, the word that is opening your mind and is renewing it unto the perfect day."

"My son, do not forget my law, but let my heart keep your commands; for length of days and long life and peace they will add to you." Proverbs 3:1-2

God says, "Faith in My word produces the greatest battle defense known to men, because faith in My word will surround you with a great, total shield, and no fiery dart will ever touch you. That is why Paul wrote to let the word of Christ dwell in you richly."

"But the Helper, the Holy Spirit, whom the Father will send in My name, He will teach you all things, and bring to your remembrance all things I said to you." John 14:26

November 15

God says, "It is never too early to teach children about the Lord. Lambs are to be nurtured with food and milk until they come into maturity."

> *"And these words which I command you today*
> *shall be in your heart; you shall teach them*
> *diligently to your children, and shall talk of*
> *them when you sit in your house, when you*
> *walk by the way, and when you rise up."*
> Deuteronomy 6:6-7

> *"We will not hide them from their children,*
> *telling to the generation to come the praises of*
> *the Lord, and His strength and His wonderful*
> *works that He has done."* Psalm 78:4

God says, "The inner man is the only place where you will find Me in your sanctuary if you begin to realize that you can reach out and touch God, for My Spirit is everywhere and knows no limitation. The word should be important to you, but the spirit assimilation of My character should also be important to you for the shaping of your soul nature, that you might be a pattern son of God."

November 16

God says, "The word of life is a sharp, two-edged sword which is able to save the soul. The saving of the soul is the saving of an individual's life pattern from the hand of the evil one. The soul of man is that part of him that was joined to the flesh before he became spirit man, and now it is joined to the Spirit by the bridge of revelation truth."

> *"...in a humble (gentle, modest) spirit receive and welcome the word which implanted and rooted [in your hearts] contains the power to save your souls."* James 1:21 (AMP)

God says, "Live in My word, and do not be troubled. Stand in My name, and do not despair."

> *"Nor is there salvation in any other, for there is no other name under heaven given among men by which we must be saved."* Acts 4:12b

November 17

God says, "Throughout the ages, men have been trying to destroy and suppress revelation knowledge, even in the institutions of religion, because they fear letting their self-kingdom go that the God-kingdom might come alive in them."

"My people are destroyed for lack of knowledge. Because you have rejected knowledge..."
Hosea 4:6

"So for the sake of your tradition... you have set aside the word of God [depriving it of force and authority and making it of no effect]."
Matthew 15:6 (AMP)

God says, "My *rhema* (spoken word) is the way to complete divorcement from the world of flesh."

To move apart from God's word is fraught with peril.

"For the word of God is living and powerful, and sharper than any two-edged sword, piercing even to the division of soul and spirit, and of joints and marrow, and is a discerner of the thoughts and intents of the heart." Hebrews 4:12

November 18

God says, "The word, *logos* (written) and *rhema* (spoken), are both one. They are both the total *rhema*. The *logos* is the *rhema* that has been revealed. The *rhema* is the *logos* that will be expanded. I do not mean for one to be taken to the detriment of the other."

"But He answered and said, 'It is written, "Man shall not live by bread alone, but by every word that proceeds from the mouth of God."'"
Matthew 4:4

"...man shall not live and be sustained by...bread alone but by every word and expression of God." Luke 4:4 (AMP)

God says, "Hear My voice within. That shall guard you, lead you, warn you, and keep you from the evil one. I urge you to let nothing stand before you and the voice of your Lord. It's My voice that leads My people through storms and trials. Be sure that the armor of God is on at all times."

"Blessed are those who hunger and thirst for righteousness, for they shall be filled." Matthew 5:6

November 19

God says, "Don't run from and don't run to evil but stand fast. Take the sword of the Spirit, the word of God, your offensive weapon, and hold your ground."

> *"Therefore take up the whole armor of God,*
> *that you may be able to withstand in the evil*
> *day, and having done all, to stand. And take*
> *the helmet of salvation, and the sword of the*
> *Spirit, which is the word of God; praying always*
> *with all prayer and supplication in the Spirit..."*
> Ephesians 6:13,17-18a

God says, "As you began to journey upon the world of the word, you found that as the word found its place within you and recreated in you a new reality, that being a man of the world no longer held the significance for you."

The word becomes our companion.

> *"The Lord will command His lovingkindness*
> *in the daytime, and in the night His song shall*
> *be with me—a prayer to the God of my life."*
> Psalm 42:8

November 20

Because God is all Spirit and we are not, we put our own input into His truth. Then we see through a glass darkly and risk wrongly dividing God's word.

"For now we see in a mirror, dimly, but then face to face. Now I know in part, but then I shall know just as I also am known."
1 Corinthians 13:12

"Be diligent to present yourself approved to God...rightly dividing the word of truth."
2 Timothy 2:15

God says, "Do not go to the right or left. Keep on the full course of the word because My words are the stepping stones by which My people walk who are seeking to walk by the Spirit."

Become a day-to-day disciple where Jesus Christ is the overriding priority for all of life's decisions.

"Establish my steps and direct them by [means of] Your word; let not any iniquity have dominion over me." Psalm 119:133 (AMP)

November 21

God says, "There's no considering another course to take, an alternative to the daily word of God within you. It's either My word or no word."

"Give me understanding, and I shall keep Your law; indeed I shall observe it with my whole heart." Psalm 119:34

"Your testimonies have I kept [hearing, receiving, loving and obeying them]; I love them exceedingly!" Psalm 119:167 (AMP)

God says, "Be faithful to see your diet contains the living word. Use My word as a catalyst to hurry you through the routine of the day so that you can find time, even in the daily routine, for the walk of the spirit man. You are bought with a price. The living word has purchased you. You are not your own!" (See 1 Corinthians 7:23.)

"Let my cry come before You, O Lord; give me understanding according to Your word. Let my supplication come before You; deliver me according to Your word." Psalm 119:169-170

November 22

The life of the Lord is in His word, but it must become alive in you—then it becomes truly living.

"I am the living bread which came down from heaven. If anyone eats of this bread, he will live forever; and the bread that I shall give is My flesh, which I shall give for the life of the world." John 6:51

God says, "Bring into captivity every thought, every deed, every action, every word—captive to the will and word of God. Walk in the holiness of My word. Walk in the truth of My word. Walk the way My Son did. Follow Him."

"...since you seek a proof of Christ speaking in me, who is not weak toward you, but mighty in you. For though He was crucified in weakness, yet He lives by the power of God. For we also are weak in Him, but we shall live with Him by the power of God toward you."
2 Corinthians 13:3-4

November 23

God says, "Be sure that you are improving yourself every time you expose yourself to My word, My walk and My way."

"Let the word [spoken by] Christ (the Messiah) have its home [in your hearts and minds] and dwell in you in [all its] richness...and whatever you do [no matter what it is] in word or deed, do everything in the name of the Lord Jesus and in [dependence upon] His person, giving praise to God always." Colossians 3:16a,17 (AMP)

God says, "I will always let you hear My word. Preserve the word. Care for it. Protect it and do not fail to nourish it, because the word is of no measurable value. It's immeasurable—the value of My word for your lives."

"This is my comfort in my affliction, for Your word has given me life." Psalm 119:50

November 24

God says, "My children, don't engage yourself in mediocrity. Don't engage yourself in the lesser things. Have done with them! I am looking for a people who will stand as a bulwark against untruth."

> *"Because of the Truth which lives and stays on*
> *in our hearts and will be with us forever: I was*
> *greatly delighted to find some of your children*
> *walking (living) in [the] truth, just as we have*
> *been commanded by the Father [Himself]."*
> 2 John 2,4 (AMP)

God says, "You have failed to live in My word's reality. Therefore, you should concentrate on that word that has not been executed in you, or you are making the word of God of none effect, and you are causing the fallen one to rejoice in that."

> *"For laying aside the commandment of God,*
> *you hold the tradition of men...making the word*
> *of God of no effect through your tradition...."*
> Mark 7:8a,13a

Traditions include old patterns of thinking and doing.

November 25

God says, "I am looking for spirit men who are going to be perfected, who will have My wisdom to understand that if they are not perfected in any area, it is because they are not about their Father's business in that area. They have neglected to let that word become part of their being."

"Not that I have already attained, or am already perfected; but I press on, that I may lay hold of that for which Christ Jesus has also laid hold of me. I press toward the goal for the prize of the upward call of God in Christ Jesus."
Philippians 3:12,14

God says, "Speak My word when you are in your spirit man, because if you speak it from your mind, My children, it is like throwing a piece of sand against a stone wall. It will not penetrate it. But when you take the sword of the Spirit, there is no force upon this earth in the natural realm that can withstand it. **Darkness must go. Disease must go. Negativity must go. Pessimism must go. Anxiety must go. Fear must go.** The sword of the Spirit penetrates because it is a spiritual weapon."

November 26

God says, "When you speak when I've not spoken, you've added to My word. But adding to My word is when you're adding to what I've not said. Taking away is when you take away what I've said otherwise; so when you take away, it's by omission."

"Whatever I command you, be careful to observe it; you shall not add to it nor take away from it." Deuteronomy 12:32

God says, "So, be cautious in uttering any vain thing before Me, saith the Lord. Let your words be few, if they are not spirit words. If they are spirit words, they can be many."

"Set a guard, O Lord, over my mouth; Keep watch over the door of my lips." Psalm 141:3

"Whoever guards his mouth and tongue keeps his soul from troubles." Proverbs 21:23

November 27

God says, "Some of you are so hungry, and My Son promised you when on this earth: 'Those that hunger and thirst after righteousness shall be filled.' I shall fill those that hunger. Those that don't hunger, I'll try to awake an appetite in you."

"So He humbled you, allowed you to hunger, and fed you with manna which you did not know nor did your fathers know, that He might make you know that man shall not live by bread alone; but man lives by every word that proceeds from the mouth of the Lord."
Deuteronomy 8:3

God says, "Feast on Me. Feast on Me and My word by My Spirit. Feast on My life that's in My word. Extract the nuggets as you meditate. Consume them deliberately, with deliberation, and not with haste."

"Your words were found, and I ate them, and Your word was to me the joy and rejoicing of my heart..." Jeremiah 15:16

"I will meditate on Your precepts, and contemplate Your ways." Psalm 119:15

November 28

God says, "Let My word be strong within you. Let My word be many within you. Let My word be as a sound of rushing waters, coming forth from your innermost being. Let My word bring you peace, joy, and love."

"He who believes in Me, as the Scripture has said, out of his heart will flow rivers of living water." John 7:38

God says, "Do you not see the value in releasing the living word that I have given you? You should know the living word in such a way that you can release it for any circumstance."

"Study and be eager and do your utmost to present yourself to God approved (tested by trial), a workman who has no cause to be ashamed, correctly analyzing and accurately dividing [rightly handling and skillfully teaching] the Word of Truth." 2 Timothy 2:15 (AMP)

"Finally, brethren, pray for us, that the word of the Lord may have free course and be glorified..." 2 Thessalonians 3:1

November 29

God says, "If you wish to dispatch the enemy of your soul, become light. Become word. Become truth. Become the new creation I speak to you to be in My *logos*."

> *"And those who belong to Christ Jesus (the Messiah) have crucified the flesh (the godless human nature) with its passions and appetites and desires. If we live by the [Holy] Spirit, let us also walk by the Spirit. [If by the Holy Spirit, we have our life in God, let us go forward walking in line, our conduct controlled by the Spirit.]"* Galatians 5:24-25 (AMP)

God says, "Let My word destroy the evil around you. Let My word be the initial wake-up call of the angels to come to stand with you, and guard and guide you, for they are assigned to be messengers, and deliverers and warriors for you."

> *"You are my hiding place and my shield; I hope in Your word. Depart from me, you evil doers, for I will keep the commandments of my God! Uphold me according to Your word, that I may live."* Psalm 119:114-116a

November 30

God says, "The man of the world cannot live in the kingdom of the man of the word, and the man of the word cannot live in the kingdom of the man of the world, for they oppose each other. The world's standards are those which corrupt. The word's standards are those which elevate."

"Because the carnal mind is enmity against God; for it is not subject to the law of God nor indeed can be. So then, those who are in the flesh cannot please God. But you are not in the flesh but in the Spirit, if indeed the Spirit of God dwells in you..." Romans 8:7-9

God says, "Life lies within you, not around you. All that is around you is fragmentary and illusionary and transient. It is a vapor. Your reality is being experienced as you enter into the kingdom, the world of the word."

"...For what is your life? It is even a vapor that appears for a little time and then vanishes away." James 4:14b

December 1

God says, "Do not give the enemy any place because he's seeking whom he may devour. Are you fully determined that only My word counts, only My way counts, only My thoughts count, and you only want to climb that spiritual ladder of maturity to go from one perfection to another in different areas of your life? That's progress. That's maturity."

> *"I will behave wisely in a perfect way. Oh, when will You come to me? I will walk within my house with a perfect heart."* Psalm 101:2

God says, "I choose to reveal things as I choose, not things you desire because you desire them, but only those things you desire that I already desire. I do not desire that which is not good for you at the time you would have Me give it to you. I give it only to those I see looking as I look and seeing as I see. It's the magnitude of your spiritual vision that determines the magnitude of My spiritual transmission."

> *"I have heard of You [only] by the hearing of the ear, but now my [spiritual] eye sees You."*
> Job 42:5 (AMP)

December 2

God says, "The word of truth should be among you. Where is the word that is mighty from the Lord? Why is it not in your mouth, for I said it's near you? And if you open your mouth, I will fill it. Do not continue to wait for something else someone else does; for I am calling on each of you to do what I've called you to do. Rise up this day, for you may not have another day to rise."

"...'But Lord, what about this man?' Jesus said to him, 'If I will that he remain till I come, what is that to you? You follow Me.'" John 21:21-22

God says, "Your mind must be shored up with the insulation of My word and My armor so that the mind of Christ might be able to forestall the enemy's beginning. It's not just the word that shores up the defenses of your temple, but your spirit in the same degree of maturity."

"Never lag in zeal and in earnest endeavor; be aglow and burning with the Spirit, serving the Lord." Romans 12:11 (AMP)

December 3

God says, "My Son is the truth giver. He is the truth standard. He is the bearer of the sword of the Spirit. In His word which He executes is love and life and health for you. He will touch you today, if you will allow Him."

"I anticipated the dawning of the morning and cried [in childlike prayer]; I hoped in Your word. My eyes anticipate the night watches and I am awake before the cry of the watchman, that I may meditate on Your word."
Psalm 119:147-148 (AMP)

God says, "My word is light and truth. My word is redemption. My word is the cleansing that will provide your mind the preparation for renewal, that I might change your thoughts, change your very soul, and recreate in you the knowledge of Me, until your soul and spirit are totally joined to My Spirit."

"Meditate on these things; give yourself entirely to them, that your progress may be evident to all." 1 Timothy 4:15

December 4

God says, "My purpose is not to draw men because I force them by My power and by My spiritual might or by miracles. My purpose is to entreat them by love of the word and love of the Spirit, for they agree. Loving that is loving Me and loving Me is to love the word and the Spirit."

"He who has My commandments and keeps them, it is he who loves Me. And he who loves Me will be loved by My Father, and I will love him and manifest Myself to him." John 14:21

God says, "The stepping stones of My word are those words that will cause you to walk on the water, as Peter did, and you will not sink. Because those stones of faith, those stones of love, those stones of greater increase of the way, the truth, and life, and resurrection, are those stones which became one stone, and that one stone will be as a lively stone composed of My elect and My Christ who is the chief cornerstone of your being."

"You also, as living stones, are being built up a spiritual house, a holy priesthood, to offer up spiritual sacrifices acceptable to God through Jesus Christ." 1 Peter 2:5

December 5

God says, "Heed My words today, My people, heed My words. They are spirit and they are life to you. I am here, don't you know? I am here, My precious ones, to comfort and lift your hearts."

"Every word of God is pure; He is a shield to those who put their trust in Him." Proverbs 30:5

"Humble yourselves [feeling very insignificant] in the presence of the Lord, and He will exalt you [He will lift you up and make your lives significant]. James 4:10 (AMP)

God says, "This is a time to subdue your mind and body, a time to recognize who you really are inside and not outside, to realize that you are inside a living epistle written by God upon tablets within your heart."

"You show and make obvious that you are a letter from Christ delivered by us, not written with ink but with [the] Spirit of [the] living God, not on tablets of stone but on tablets of human hearts." 2 Corinthians 3:3 (AMP)

December 6

Faith is a present principle. Faith is an ever present help in time of trouble.

"For we walk by faith, not by sight."
2 Corinthians 5:7

"Fight the good fight of faith, lay hold on eternal life, to which you were also called and have confessed the good confession in the presence of many witnesses." 1 Timothy 6:12

God says, "Faith is a conviction that that which appears contrary to God or contrary to what you are anticipating in the Spirit is nonexistent, and the only reality is Spirit and truth."

"...Not being weak in faith, he did not consider his own body, already dead (since he was about a hundred years old), and the deadness of Sarah's womb. He did not waver at the promise of God through unbelief, but was strengthened in faith, giving glory to God, and being fully convinced that what He had promised He was also able to perform." Romans 4:19-21

December 7

God says, "Faith cannot be exercised in bondage."

Faith cannot be exercised when the spirit is not free.

Habits are so slowly lost because we have habits that we think give us freedom from the word of God. This happens when we reach out beyond what God gives us.

> *"Now the Lord is the Spirit, and where the*
> *Spirit of the Lord is, there is liberty (emancipa-*
> *tion from bondage, freedom)."*
> 2 Corinthians 3:17 (AMP)

Faith will always focus on the Lord. When we compare Goliath to ourselves, he will be too powerful. When we compare Goliath to God, Goliath is powerless.

> *"And all the men of Israel, when they saw*
> *Goliath, fled from him and were dreadfully*
> *afraid. Then David spoke to the men and said,*
> *'Who is this uncircumcised Philistine, that he*
> *should defy the armies of the living God?'"*
> 1 Samuel 17:24,26b

December 8

God says, "Doubt may not sink you, but when fear goes with doubt, that will sink you."

> *"...and when Peter had come down out of the boat, he walked on the water to go to Jesus. But when he saw that the wind was boisterous, he was afraid; and beginning to sink he cried out, saying, 'Lord, save me!' And immediately Jesus stretched out His hand and caught him, and said to him, 'O you of little faith, why did you doubt?'"* Matthew 14:29-31

Doubt cancels faith, but faith cancels doubt!

God says, "Doubt is the enemy of faith. Doubt says, 'I can't quite get it. I can't quite believe it. I'm not certain, but I believe in my mind it's true. I can't convince my heart.' Doubt says, 'I know God exists. I know He can do it; but if it's His will, He'll do it.'"

Satan is always there to convince you that God's word is not true. He plants the question, "Has God indeed said?" (See Genesis 3:1.)

> *"So Jesus answered and said to them, 'Assuredly, I say to you, if you have faith and do not doubt, you will not only do what was done to the fig tree, but also if you say to this mountain, 'Be removed and be cast into the sea,' it will be done."* Matthew 21:21

December 9

Trust is the birth of faith. Faith is saying amen to the spirit realm. Faith is certainty you know it's done.

God says, "Doubt and trust do not mix. You must trust Me for circumstances you're in doubt about. I'm with you. Do not doubt."

Doubt does not come from God, for God did not create doubt. Doubt is a product of the enemy.

> *"I have fought the good fight, I have finished the race, I have kept the faith."* 2 Timothy 4:7-8

God says, "Raise that hedge of protection and revelation knowledge and faith by praying in the spirit and by praise and meditation. Doubt is a forerunner of the enemy coming in to strike. You must not let your guard down."

> *"But you, beloved, building yourselves up on your most holy faith, praying in the Holy Spirit, keep yourselves in the love of God..."* Jude 20-21

December 10

An evil report can come to us through another person or through an imagination. An evil report is intended to destroy our faith and trust in God.

> *"Then Caleb quieted the people before Moses, and said, 'Let us go up at once and take posses-sion, for we are well able to overcome it.' But the men who had gone up with him said, 'We are not able to go up against the people, for they are stronger than we.' And they gave the chil-dren of Israel a bad report...and the people wept that night [and said], 'Why has the Lord brought us to this land to fall by the sword...'"*
> Numbers 13:30-32a, 14:1b,3

God says, "Without faith you cannot please Me, the faith to know that God is with you in whatever situation you are in. I am grieved that so many times in your life you've attempted to do things, thinking it was up to you to do them, and you do not realize it's My desire to do them because I see the desire in you comes from your spirit."

> *"For since the beginning of the world men have not heard nor perceived by the ear, nor has the eye seen any God besides You, Who acts for the one who waits for Him."* Isaiah 64:4

December 11

God asks, "Is the control of My Lordship to the point where you will not question anything I say, but you will do it gladly with abandonment? You will not pick and choose what you will hear, receive, or grow into in terms of giving your life to Me."

> *"Take heed to yourself and to the doctrine. Continue in them, for in doing this you will save both yourself and those who hear you."*
> 1 Timothy 4:16

God says, "My joy in you comes when you know I am in charge of your life. And when I know you have given Me charge of your entire life, I can do so much that you can't even believe what I can do for you."

> *"If you keep My commandments, you will abide in My love, just as I have kept My Father's commandments and abide in His love. These things I have spoken to you, that My joy may remain in you, and that your joy may be full."*
> John 15:10-11

December 12

Christ is the only voice in creation that God listens to. The Father is not interested in earthly words. We must speak the words of Christ. God does hear the cry of faith from the spirit. He still speaks today in the hearts of His people.

"For He whom God has sent speaks the words of God, for God does not give the Spirit by measure." John 3:34

"...But whatever is given you in that hour, speak that; for it is not you who speak, but the Holy Spirit." Mark 13:11b

God says, "You must believe My word more than you believe anything else in this entire world. You must actually take My promises and believe them until the point where you are willing to live and die on those promises. Then you will see My faith work in your life, and then nothing shall stand before you."

[And Nebuchadnezzar said to the three Hebrew children,] "And who is the god who will deliver you from my hands?" [And they answered,] "If that is the case, our God whom we serve is able to deliver us from the burning fiery furnace, and He will deliver us from your hand, O king."
Daniel 3:15c,17

December 13

Don't ask God for something when you may want to wait and test your faith with Him instead. God is waiting to see a man of faith in this earth rise up.

"But He [Jesus] said, 'The things which are impossible with men are possible with God.'"
Luke 18:27

"Behold, I am the Lord, the God of all flesh. Is there anything too hard for Me?" Jeremiah 32:27

God says, "My God shall meet all my needs, as the apostle said, through His riches in glory, by Christ Jesus. I would tell you that I am meeting people's needs who will need Me more than they need anything else, even the necessary food they put in their bodies. If they need Me more than they need their own paycheck, then they need Me rightly."

"I have not departed from the commandment of His lips; I have treasured the words of His mouth more than my necessary food." Job 23:12

December 14

God says, "My actions do not include disease. My will for you is not to be sick. My will for you all is not to carry anything within your body that was not created to be in there."

"Beloved, I pray that you may prosper in all things and be in health, just as your soul prospers."
3 John 2

The soul cannot prosper until the spirit prospers.

God says, "I will heal physically after I have given your spirit total health. Then the mind and body will follow. It should not be the reverse fashion."

"'Return, you backsliding children, and I will heal your backslidings.' 'Indeed we do come to You, for You are the Lord our God.'" Jeremiah 3:22

"But to you who fear My name the Sun of Righteousness shall arise with healing in His wings; and you shall go out and grow fat like stall-fed calves." Malachi 4:2

December 15

God says, "Healing is not a gift. Healing is your right to life in Me. Healing is My privilege, and I desire to keep you in health. Healing is your birthright in Christ. It's your birthright in maturity. When your soul is right, the health will flow."

"Bless the Lord, O my soul, and forget not all His benefits: Who forgives all your iniquities, Who heals all your diseases, Who redeems your life from destruction, Who crowns you with lovingkindness and tender mercies, Who satisfies your mouth with good things, so that your youth is renewed like the eagle's." Psalm 103:2-5

God says, "My Son has already left the virtue of healing on this earth. He not only carried your sins but your pains, diseases, and sickness—by whose stripes you were healed. That is the faith of Romans 4:17. He called those things that be not as though they were. You were healthy, you are healthy, and every present moment of the present moment you will be healthy, as I am that I am will always be I am that I am. Your weakness is My strength, My opportunity to insert My strength in that area of your body that needs strengthening."

December 16

God has addressed the characteristics a person needs that will allow God to change him:

1. A meek and willing spirit
2. A meek and willing soul
3. A meek and willing will
4. A meek and willing heart

Our confession: "I am willing to be made willing to conform to the complete and perfect will of God in my life."

> *"My heart is breaking with the longing that it has for Your ordinances and judgments at all times. I have inclined my heart to perform Your statues forever, even to the end."*
> Psalm 119:20,112 (AMP)

God says, "It takes a strong man to admit he needs God."

> *"...The Lord is the strength of my life; of whom shall I be afraid?"* Psalm 27:1b

> *"With my soul I have desired You in the night, yes, by my spirit within me I will seek You early..."* Isaiah 26:9a

December 17

God says, "My Spirit is a Spirit that changes and makes a sinner a saint, and makes a saint the meekest man on earth."

"But the fruit of the Spirit is love, joy, peace, longsuffering, kindness, goodness, faithfulness, gentleness, self-control. Against such there is no law." Galatians 5:22-23

God says, "The Lord is calling everyone to relieve themselves of a proud and haughty heart, for meekness is the name of Christ, and without meekness and holiness, no man shall ever see God."

"He leads the humble in what is right, and the humble He teaches His way." Psalm 25:9 (AMP)

"Pursue peace with all people, and holiness, without which no one will see the Lord." Hebrews 12:14

December 18

God says, "My beloved one, keep reaching for Me, for you will find Me in a quiet place, and I'll be there waiting for you, so be ready to receive Me in your heart. Be ready to come with Me through this life's way. Through every day and every night My voice shall speak to you, and you'll hear Me if you quiet your outer man. When We meet together in the quiet place, I will speak to you and show you things I planned for Us when We are in eternity."

"...you stand still, first, that I may cause you to hear the word of God." 1 Samuel 9:27b (AMP)

God says, "Be still and know that I am God. You can't be noisy and know that I am God. I don't want to hear your voice. I want to hear My voice in your heart and have you reflect on it."

"...I will...stand upon my post of observation and station myself on the tower or fortress, and will watch to see what He will say within me..."
Habakkuk 2:1 (AMP)

December 19

God says, "Reach out and touch Me and let Me touch your life with My hand."

"For I know the thoughts that I think toward you, says the Lord, thoughts of peace and not of evil, to give you a future and a hope. Then you will call upon Me and go and pray to Me, and I will listen to you. And you will seek Me and find Me, when you search for Me with all your heart." Jeremiah 29:11-13

God says, "Lean to those things your heart finds music to and feels drawn to and a bond, and a commonality with—that's God's Holy Spirit."

"Now there are diversities of gifts, but the same Spirit. There are differences of ministries, but the same Lord. And there are diversities of activities, but it is the same God who works all in all. But one and the same Spirit works all these things, distributing to each one individually as He wills." 1 Corinthians 12:4-6,11

December 20

God says, "You must have that pleasure of communication with Me regularly because you need it."

> *"Give ear to my words, O Lord, consider my*
> *meditation. Give heed to the voice of my cry,*
> *my King and my God, for to You I will pray.*
> *My voice You shall hear in the morning,*
> *O Lord; in the morning I will direct it to You,*
> *and I will look up."* Psalm 5:1-3

God says, "The thing I want to do now is have you sit under My Spirit and learn sweet communion with Me. I want to see your spirits enter the rest God has prepared for His people. Learn of Me, for I will give rest to your souls."

> *"...Martha welcomed Him into her house. And*
> *she had a sister called Mary, who also sat at*
> *Jesus' feet and heard His word. But Martha*
> *was distracted with much serving...and Jesus*
> *answered and said to her, 'Martha, Martha,*
> *you are worried and troubled about many*
> *things. But one thing is needed, and Mary has*
> *chosen that good part, which will not be taken*
> *away from her.'"* Luke 10:38b-40a,41-42

Martha did not understand that the God Who can call manna down from heaven was her guest.

December 21

God says, "Do not quench the Spirit. When the Spirit is quenched, He is not in fellowship with your spirit. When the Spirit of God is not in communion with you, your spirit cannot have communion at all."

"The grace of the Lord Jesus Christ, and the love of God, and the communion of the Holy Spirit be with you all. Amen."
2 Corinthians 13:14

God says, "The window of your soul is what looks out on God and tries to reason. The door in your heart is one that is finally open forever. Christ doesn't close the door. He opens the door for you. He has intimacy to His presence, to His love, and you begin to see that what He is, is what you will be in the eternities of eternities to come."

"...these things says He who is holy, He who is true...He who opens and no one shuts, and shuts and no one opens." Revelation 3:7

December 22

God says, "Stay with just one morsel of My truth and think on it. Put it in your thoughts. Speak it. Savor it. Taste it and see that the Lord is good and begin to be quiet."

"All ate the same spiritual food, and all drank the same spiritual drink. For they drank of that spiritual Rock that followed them, and that Rock was Christ." 1 Corinthians 10:3-4

God says, "Many are choosing, picking and choosing, those things of the written word that are convenient for them. They are choosing to ignore those things of the written word that are necessary."

Studying the word prepares you for the day. It allows the truth to insulate your heart, but remember this—the word does not yield its fruit to those who approach it lazily. All fruit takes time to ripen.

"Oh, how I love Your law! It is my meditation all the day." Psalm 119:97

December 23

God says, "Shut yourself off in a quiet place. Come into your bedchamber and seek Me, and I shall reveal Myself to you. Come into your spirit. Come into your spirit man, for Christ is within you, your hope of glory. Come up, rise up, and see the glory of God."

"Come, My people, enter your chambers, and shut your doors behind you; hide yourself, as it were, for a little moment, until the indignation is past." Isaiah 26:20

God says, "You must keep your warmth and love for Me. You must have a walk with Me, and you must talk with Me in the quiet of your night. You must spend time talking with Me from your heart."

"...Meditate within your heart on your bed, and be still. Selah" Psalm 4:4b

"When I remember You on my bed, I meditate on You in the night watches. My soul follows close behind You; Your right hand upholds me."
Psalm 63:6,8

December 24

God asks, "Why did I call you perfect, call you to perfection if you are not going to do it? Why did I call you to live like my Son unless you can do it—to have His mind and to take your authority over spiritual rulers of darkness in the high places? If you cannot do it, why would I say it? Why would I call you to cast out demons if you cannot do it? Why did I call you to heal the sick if you cannot do it?"

> *"And these signs will follow those who believe:*
> *In My name they will cast out demons; they*
> *will speak with new tongues; they will lay hands*
> *on the sick, and they will recover."* Mark 16:17-18

God says, "When a man is in Christ in body, mind, and spirit, he's a new creation. You can be Christ in spirit, and not be Christ in mind. You can be Christ in spirit, and not be Christ in body. You can be Christ in spirit, and not be Christ in body and mind both; but they are not able to overcome the spirit."

> *"That which is born of flesh is flesh, and that*
> *which is born of the Spirit is spirit."* John 3:6

December 25

God says, "It will take My finishing completion to perfect you. I shall perfect that which concerns you, but you must strive for the mark of the high calling, that every thought you think, every deed you do, every act you walk in, shall be as though Christ were walking in you, through you, and with you."

> *"Being confident of this very thing, that He who has begun a good work in you will complete it until the day of Jesus Christ."* Philippians 1:6

> *"...work out your own salvation with fear and trembling; for it is God who works in you both to will and to do for His good pleasure."*
> Philippians 2:12b-13

God says, "It's just this, My children. Pleasing Satan is easy. Pleasing Me is not easy, and I will not apologize for making it so high a standard for you. I said the way to life is narrow and straight, the gate straight, and few there be that go thereon."

> *"That you may walk (live and conduct yourselves) in a manner worthy of the Lord, fully pleasing to Him and desiring to please Him in all things..."* Colossians 1:10a (AMP)

December 26

God says, "Jesus Christ comes to renew your heart and faith today. He comes to show you there is a better way. Jesus Christ brings heaven to earth and casts out earth in you. He brings truth you have not heard—revelation that will finish your perfection."

Do not be careless or sleepy or apathetic when He comes.

> *"Therefore you shall be perfect, just as your Father in heaven is perfect."* Matthew 5:48

Maranatha, even so, come quickly, Lord Jesus.

God says, "I am love. I love love. I love joy. I love peace. I love tranquility. I love order. I love direction. I love My kingdom. I am the One Who will radically change your earth nature to become a kingdom of perfection, a kingdom of truth, and I love truth."

> *"Peter said to Him, …'You shall never wash my feet!' Jesus answered him, 'If I do not wash you, you have no part with Me.'"* John 13:8

December 27

Christ Jesus says, "I want you to be satisfied with your walk and not have anything to apologize for before My Father, because My Father is a zealous Father Who will hold you to a higher standard than you may think, and I told you not to be perfect like Me, but to be perfect like My Father in heaven." (See Matthew 5:48.)

> *"You will show me the path of life; in Your presence is fullness of joy; at Your right hand are pleasures forevermore."* Psalm 16:11

> *"Who may ascend into the hill of the Lord? Or who may stand in His holy place? He who has clean hands and a pure heart, who has not lifted up his soul to an idol, nor sworn deceitfully."* Psalm 24:3-4

You are not to compare yourself with one another. You are to compare yourself only with God so that you can strive toward His standard.

> *"...However, when they measure themselves with themselves and compare themselves with one another, they are without understanding and behave unwisely."* 2 Corinthians 10:12b (AMP)

December 28

God says, "I will open new doors and new avenues for you. Flow in them without fear or anxiety, for I will show you new things. I will use you to do My work. As you minister in the areas I've chosen for you, do so with a holy boldness. Walk in the Spirit. Do not be afraid of the enemy. He shall avail nothing."

> *"Look, the Lord your God has set the land before you; go up and possess it, as the Lord God of your fathers has spoken to you; do not fear or be discouraged."* Deuteronomy 1:21

God says, "When the Holy Spirit brings the anointing, what you do with it determines what the anointing will do with you in the future."

> *"In His love and in His pity He redeemed them; and He bore them and carried them all the days of old. But they rebelled and grieved His Holy Spirit; so He turned Himself against them as an enemy."* Isaiah 63:9b–10a

December 29

God says, "Consider the ways of the Lord. He sleeps not, neither does He slumber. In the times when He's given His beloved rest, think not that He is resting. But He works that that work might be the bringing into fruition of the kingdom of God upon this earth."

"He will not allow your foot to be moved; He who keeps you will not slumber. Behold, He who keeps Israel shall neither slumber nor sleep." Psalm 121:3-4

"Let us therefore be diligent to enter that rest..." Hebrews 4:11a

God says, "I am all things to all people who will yield to My word. My word will set you free and heal you. My word will cause you to be stirred up where you cannot think of anything but God, your God, your loyal Father, the Father Who will come when you're in trouble, the Father Who will send His angels when you're in need, the Father Who will send His Son when all is ready."

December 30

God says, "From this moment on I don't want you to trust yourself in any area. Give it up to Me, children, and live. Give it up right now, children. Just be willing and relinquish it now. Don't trust yourself from this moment on. Just admit that you can't trust yourself. You just go in a circle with your mind. You get in a trap, and the enemy's given you that trap."

"He who trusts in his own heart is a fool. But whoever walks wisely will be delivered."
Proverbs 28:26

God says, "I have no pleasure in My children who are satisfied, who are satisfied and who remain hindered by the status quo; for My children are a peculiar treasure, and I desire that they advance in the kingdom. There is no place in the kingdom or the economy of God for people being self-satisfied."

December 31

God says, "He shall give treasures to those who are faithful to the keeping of those treasures, those who will answer Him and receive Him and trust Him. Yea, as He gives treasures unto you, He knows your hearts; and He knows that where your treasure is, is your heart. Yea, indeed, if you have treasure upon this earth, how can you have treasure in the heaven if this treasure upon this earth stands between you and the real treasure?"

"But lay up for yourselves treasures in heaven, where neither moth nor rust destroys and where thieves do not break in and steal, for where your treasure is, there your heart will be also."
Matthew 6:20-21

God says, "These things that I have given you, the treasures of My heart, are those things of value which you need to invest your life in. Know ye not that when you invest your life in these treasures, I will let them sparkle as gold in your heart and in your life. Those treasures which I give are My gift of love. Receive Me as the greatest treasure that you could ever possess. I am a treasure that cannot be bought."

Sound of Many Waters
Order Form

Postal orders: 5187 Knotty Pine Lane
Evergreen, CO 80439

Telephone orders: 303-674-2096

E-mail orders: patti7777@msn.com

Please send *Sound of Many Waters* to:

Name: ____

Address: ____

City: _____________________________ State: ______________

Zip: _______________ Telephone: (______) ________________

Book Price: $17.99

Shipping: $3.00 for the first book and $1.00 for each additional book to cover shipping and handling within US, Canada, and Mexico. International orders add $6.00 for the first book and $2.00 for each additional book.

Or order from:

ACW Press
P.O. Box 110390
Nashville, TN 37222

(800) 931-BOOK

or contact your local bookstore